D1413475

Authority and Participation in Industry

Work and Society in the Eighties

Series Editor: Michael Rose
Senior Lecturer, School of Humanities and Social Sciences
and
Centre for European Industrial Studies, University of Bath

This series aims to present authoritative treatments of key aspects of work, in its role as a central social and historical phenomenon in human life. All volumes are written by specialists in the appropriate fields, but in such a way that together they will provide interlocking coverage of concepts, controversies, and major trends in a variety of academic subject areas concerned with work issues. At the same time, they supply valuable documentation on the movement of values, action and structures in advanced societies in general. Students will find the series especially helpful, but it will also challenge professionals in management and industrial relations to review their own practice, provide teachers and researchers with stimulating new interpretations, and come to the aid of general readers wishing to be fully informed about the subject.

In preparation:

Class at Work:
the Design, Allocation
and Control of Jobs
Craig Littler and Graeme Salaman

AUTHORITY AND PARTICIPATION IN INDUSTRY

PETER BRANNEN

St. Martin's Press · New York

For Alex and Emil

Printed in Great Britain by Billing & Sons Ltd, Worcester

First published in the United States of America in 1983

ISBN 0-312-06123-4

Library of Congress Cataloging in Publication Data

Brannen, Peter.
    Authority and participation in industry.

    Bibliography: p.
    Includes index.
    1. Industrial management — Great Britain — Employee
participation.   2. Industrial management — Employee
participation I. Title
HD5660.G7B675 1983   658.3' 152   83-16151

ISBN 0-312-06123-4

Contents

Editor's Foreword

Currently – but for how long? – the movement for work democracy as an officially promoted institutional innovation is out of fashion in most countries. Yet 'participation' and 'worker involvement' are terms endlessly repeated by management professionals. This is as true for the United States, where the campaign for institutionalised industrial democracy has never been strong, as for Western Europe, where European Community law seems slowly to be swinging behind democratisation of the workplace. On both sides of the Atlantic, though, 'participative' devices like the *autonomous working group* or the *quality circle* are in vogue.

This may bewilder those tough-minded politicians who believe high unemployment should solve workplace problems. High unemployment certainly cuts the strike-rate and curbs blatant insubordination. But it does nothing to make increasingly better educated workers positively committed to work organisations which they often perceive as greedy and intrusive. It does nothing to make them eager to produce a work performance that will do more than scrape past a supervisor or inspector.

As far as the United States goes, the trends which such different observers as Rosabeth Kanter, Daniel Yankelovitch, and Charles Heckscher have delineated seem likely to be sustained over the longer term: the politics of nostalgia may be having their turn in the White House; in the American workplace, the politics of organisational civil rights and 'New Breed' values will go on creating a climate that should favour work democracy over the longer term. It is noticeable, in fact, that one of the longest-running and most often reported work reform experiments in the USA, at the Tarrytown, New York, plant of General Motors, always incorporated a large slice of formalised worker participation; this should have been better noticed than it has been in both countries.

In Britain, an aggressive approach to questions of authority in the workplace is thought to be much admired amongst leaders of the current administration. Paradoxically, though, amongst the 'tougher' professional managers who have recently been emerging in British industry a favourite phrase seems to be: 'Muscle is out!'

Such claims need to be taken with a pinch of salt. Yet research on work reorganisation being undertaken by the present writer and a colleague indicates that whilst there has been concern to limit union influence on

British shopfloors, managers are genuinely concerned not merely to avoid provoking reaction through heavy-handedness but also to achieve greater involvement by employees. Not many believe this can be achieved by purely cosmetic measures. For such reasons, work democracy remains on the agenda. In addition, the modern electoral volatility of Britain could suddenly produce a swing that reversed current government policies on the question well before the end of the decade.

It is difficult to conceive of a work reform that would mark a historic change more decisively than a clear move in such a direction. Soviet, Western, and 'post-Confucian' organisations share a fundamentally similar hierarchic structure. In none of these systems is there an effective civil right giving employees a say in policies that deeply affect their lives. Thus, in some countries, subnormal citizens have the right to help choose political leaders who hold the power to vaporise humanity; but highly trained employees are not trusted to help make such decisions as whether to instal an organisational creche. There is something weird about societies with priorities like that.

Possibly the current decade will see some real movement towards greater trust and involvement of employees by organisations. Whatever happens, the central *ideas* of worker democracy will continue to feed debates on the structure of employment relationships and economic society as a whole.

It is with such core issues that this series will be concerned. The aim of the authors is, firstly, to give central issues a focused treatment rather than to pursue encyclopaedic coverage; secondly, not to fight shy of saying what they really think about the issues but to hold in check any impulse to indulge in polemics.

Peter Brannen's book is the first volume of the series. He has carefully avoided writing a typical book on participation. Readers who know The Typical Book on Participation will be grateful. The latter is a nightmare for anybody who really wants to learn something about the question. Its favourite method is to itemise undigested facts, seemingly chosen half at random, about the work democracy movement in several countries. But such supposedly 'comparative' approaches leave no clear picture about what has been occurring in any given country and becloud awareness of the extent to which some international trend may exist.

Instead, Brannen has given priority to the British case, introducing material from other societies only when such comparison can be telling. In this way, the hopes, apprehensions, and dilemmas surrounding greater work democracy that occur everywhere are brought to life by showing the detailed shape they have taken in one national case. The author is ideally equipped for the task he has set himself. In particular, he has a first-hand knowledge of worker democracy as practical politics in Britain. When the British Steel Corporation undertook an experiment with employee-elected worker directors in the seventies, Brannen acted as Leading Investigator on the evaluation study of the scheme sponsored by the Social Science Research

Council. Subsequently he has been responsible for conceiving and overseeing a programme of research on worker participation which has been conducted at a number of research institutions in the United Kingdom. His experience is used effectively in the text.

It is, however, for readers to make up their minds about the book. The same goes for the series as a whole. We have the firm intention of developing it in ways that successfully meet the needs of our readers. Reactions, comments, or suggestions that readers believe will help us to do so will be very welcome to us, and can be sent either to the publisher, or to the Series Editor at the address below.

Michael Rose
University of Bath

Preface

Throughout the evolution of industrial society, participation and the exercise of control by workers in the enterprises in which they work has been a major ideological and practical issue. The issue persists because, as John Corina put it, 'it is the cry of a deep-seated human need. Where that need is denied – in the Communist system or in the West – the undercurrents of frustration boil over into political discontent.' We have seen a resurgence of interest in participation bubble to the surface over large parts of Western Europe in the 1960s; and in Eastern Europe increased participation a central demand of the Polish Solidarity trade union movement. Within the European Community worker participation remains on the political agenda and in Britain, despite severe recession, it continues to be included in the manifestos and policy proposals of the main political parties. A recent article addressed to management sees 'a real prospect of measures for industrial participation being introduced into the United Kingdom in response to political pressures, internal or external, rather than the pragmatic reasons based on practical industrial experience', but – commenting on a proposal for a national framework within which companies could map out their own arrangements – suggests also that time is running out (IPA, 1982).

The continuing interest in worker participation has led to a proliferation of books and articles on the topic. However, whilst students are increasingly well served in the areas of institutional description, prescription, and analysis, it is also the case that to a great degree the literature on worker participation exists in a vacuum, independent of much writing in social theory and social history and in the general fields of industrial sociology and political economy. The aim of this text is to go some little way towards correcting this, to set some of the literature on worker participation alongside these other literatures and, by placing a diverse range of material within the same covers, to help the reader to make new connections. Whilst a large part of the material in the book is derived from Britain, the issues which it illustrates, whether these be the dynamics of boardroom participation, the uneven development of participatory institutions or the relationship between market segmentation and worker participation, are intended to have a broader application. Where the British experience or the British literature is inadequate, material from other countries has been used. In addition both the bibliography at the end of the book and the sections on further reading concluding each chapter refer to comparative material.

A number of people have provided support and critical comment during the process of writing. I am grateful to Julia Brannen for her agreement, under protest, to extend our contract over the weekend domestic division of labour so that I could complete this text. Eric Batstone, Fred Bayliss, Richard Brown, John Eldrige, Bill Hawes, Michael Rose and Tony Seward gave me help and criticism in a variety of ways and I am indebted to them. I also need to thank Brian Towers, Ray Loveridge, and Eric Batstone for allowing me to quote from material which was unpublished when this text went to press. Needless to say neither those mentioned above nor my employing organisation are responsible for the deficiencies of the manuscript nor for any views or interpretations it contains.

Peter Brannen
Ealing, London
January 1983

Introduction

This book focuses on the participation of workers in the power, authority and control structures of the organisations in which they work. Most people, both women and men, spend a major portion of their lifetimes as part of the labour force, selling their labour power in exchange for income. For women, high participation over the working lifetime is particularly the case in the UK but the trend in other industrialised countries is in a similar direction (Manley and Sawbridge, 1980). Within the world of employment, most people have neither the formal rights nor the freedom and control which they have within their domestic, community and political lives. Industrial democracy is a less developed notion than political democracy. Employment takes place within organisations where the activities of the individual are formally subject to a contract, the specific terms of which are vague but which in a general sense puts her or his labour power or work capacity at the disposition of the employer. The control and co-ordination of this labour power in a specific way has been seen to require the exercise of authority through hierarchical structures. The balance between worker control and employer authority has been contested terrain throughout the development of industrial society (Brown, 1981, p. 225). This is the case, though to varying degrees, whether the employer is capital, the state, or labour itself as in co-operative or self management systems.

During the last two decades increasing interest has been expressed by politicians, intellectuals, and industrial relations practitioners in the issue of worker participation and industrial democracy. Historically also, though under a variety of labels, the subject has been a major intellectual preoccupation for social theorists and analysts, and a major practical one for workers of all kinds and those who organise and control their labour. Indeed one of the problems which confronts anyone writing in this area is the variety of meanings given to terms such as 'worker participation' and 'industrial democracy'. They are loosely used in common parlance, sometimes in an interchangeable way, but sometimes also to denote an ideological stance towards the issues under review. They imply that individuals or groups may influence, control, be involved in, exercise power within, or be able to intervene in decision-making within organisations. Each of these indicates varying degrees of intensity; for example, the term 'influence' indicates a lower degree of intensity of participation than the term 'control'; sometimes the degree of intensity is not indicated. 'Participation' is also used to imply interaction at different organisational levels from the work group to the board room, by different groups of actors, workers or sometimes management, over different issue areas (pace of work, capital investment programmes), and through different institutional structures (work group meetings, collective bargaining). It is also used to indicate different objectives with different underpinnings; thus for some writers and analysts the purposes of participation are related to economic or organisational efficiency, for others to workplace humanisation, for yet others to self-determination. All these usages relate to participation in organisational management. 'Economic' participation relates to worker involvement in the *ownership* of organisations.

Roca and Retour have analysed the use made of the term 'participation' by 30 different authors and concluded that 'there is no agreement as to what are the dimensions of participation and furthermore within each dimension there exist marked discrepancies of treatment' (Roca and Retour, 1981). Pateman has also criticised the way in which the terms 'participation' and 'industrial democracy' are used in the literature to indicate a variety of different activities, from providing information to employees to forms of self determination (Pateman, 1970). She suggests that using the term 'participation' to cover management techniques for keeping workers informed or persuading them to accept particular decisions is to misuse it. Participation must, she argues, 'be participation *in* something'; and in the context of industry it must refer to involvement in decision-making. Activities which involve one-way information passing or discussion for therapeutic or persuasive reasons she terms 'pseudo participation' and argues that much of the activity of the human relations and neo-human relations writers and practitioners can be classified in this way (p. 89-96). One problem, however, is that it is difficult, simply by looking at the shape of institutions or procedures externally, to know whether participation in an active sense is taking place. Some institutions which have a formal participative goal become or operate as institutions of 'pseudo participation'; other institutions which are set up on the basis of pseudo participation can, in fact, become participatory.

The notion of participation *in* decision making is, however, itself also problematic. It can include both the ability to influence something and the ability to determine the outcome. These are very different things. Workers in certain situations may be able to have a say in outcomes without in any way altering management's ability finally to decide things. In other situations management may not be able to act without the agreement of the workforce. Pateman refers to a situation where one party can influence a decision but does not have equal power to decide outcomes as 'partial participation'. Full participation, by contrast, is 'the process by which each individual member of a decision-making body has equal power to determine the outcome of decisions' (p. 71). For individual members it should also be possible to substitute groups or collectivities. In this sense full participation can refer to the activities of autonomous work groups or to joint decision-making by unions and management over a company's investment programme.

Participation can indeed take place over different issues and at different points in the structure of the organisation. Abrahamsson has made a broad distinction between 'political participation', that is 'involvement in high level goal setting and long-term planning' and 'socio-technical' participation, that is 'involvement in the organisation's production' (Abrahamsson, 1977, p. 189). Political participation is primarily effective in extending the role for employees in management; it affects both what he calls the mandator role, that is those responsible for setting up or financing the organisation, and the executive role. Political participation will also affect the organisation's environment 'as it will involve the rise to power of (partly) different interests.' (p. 189). Socio-technical participation, on the other hand, extends the workers' involvement in production, that is the implementation of decisions taken at a higher level. Abrahamsson sees the changes which follow from this as internal to the organisation, thus not affecting the role of the mandator group or the long-term role of the organisation.

Participation at these two levels can however be either partial or full, in Pateman's terms. She points out that 'not only is it possible for partial participation at both management levels to take place without a democratisation of authority structures but it is also possible for full participation to be introduced at the lower level within the context of a non-democratic structure over-all' (p. 73). Partial participation at the political level may well have only minor implications for the mandator role whereas full participation is likely to have much more profound implications. She reserves the term 'industrial democracy' for full participation by employees at the political level of the enterprise.

In her discussion Pateman tends to use the terms 'authority' and 'power' interchangeably. There are however important distinctions between the terms. Weber defined power as 'the probability that one actor within a social relationship will be in a position to carry out his own will despite resistance regardless of the basis on which the probability rests' (Weber, 1979, p. 53). Authority is a subset of this, whereby obedience is produced because a subordinate accepts the superordinate's right to command as legitimate. Other subsets of power can also be defined. 'Coercion' refers to a situation where compliance is gained through the threat of deprivation or through actual deprivation. 'Influence' refers to a situation where one person causes another to change their action without recourse to command or tacit or overt threat. Finally, 'manipulation' is a category in which one actor complies without recognising either the source or the exact nature of the demand made upon him. All the above categories refer to individual action but are equally applicable to collective action. The definitions refer to the active production of compliance; but power can also be exercised by preventing something from happening (Lukes, 1974).

Workers' participation is about the distribution and exercise of power, in all its manifestations, between the owners and managers of organisations and those employed by them. It refers to the direct involvement of individuals in decisions relating to their immediate work organisation and to indirect involvement in decision-making, through representatives, in the wider socio-technical and political structures of the firm. It encompasses a variety of institutional structures, such as collective bargaining, joint consultation, workers' councils, autonomous work groups, and their operation, as well as less formal practices. Within this book the focus is largely on the institutions of indirect or representative participation and the factors that affect its operation, at both the socio-technical and political levels of the enterprise.

The book sets out to explore the operation of worker participation, the processes surrounding it and the development of these processes within industrial market society. It concentrates in large part on the British experience but ranges more widely where this is necessary. The notion of worker participation is complex; in explaining its operation it is necessary to include a wide range of variables and to draw on historical experience as well as on material from the general fields of industrial sociology, industrial relations and political economy. In doing so the intention has not been to present new data but, by including a diverse range of evidence within the same covers, to help the reader to make new connections. Whilst all market societies have faced similar problems in the course of their development both the intensity of these problems and institutional reaction to them have varied; variation has been contingent on economic and technical forces, political and cultural traditions, the structure of industrial relations and the relative power of the principal categories of actors within this structure. The British experience provides a specific case within which to understand the general social processes which relate to worker participation at both the macro and micro levels.

The first chapter outlines a number of conceptual themes which are relevant to a consideration of worker participation, introducing material that will be examined in more detail in subsequent chapters. The next chapter looks at the ebb and flow of interest in and pressure for a variety of forms of worker participation in Britain since the early part of the nineteenth century. This sets up a perspective from which to view the attitudes towards, and developments in, worker participation during the post-1945 period, which make up the substance of the following chapters. Chapter Three outlines the main patterns of economic and industrial change in Britain in the post-war period, their implications for relationships between labour and management, and the institutional response, both at the level of the state and that of the firm. The period from the mid-1960s saw a surge of public interest in a variety of forms of worker participation; we examine the main developments but concentrate in the final part of the chapter on the less public but substantial growth in institutions of joint consultation. The following two chapters examine workers' (and their representatives') and managements' attitudes towards participation. Chapter Four examines sociological theorising on worker motivation and work orientations and relates this to attitudes towards worker participation. In particular it focuses on the implications of community, work and market situation for workers' aspirations towards and ability to be involved in participatory systems. It then examines recent empirical evidence on workers' orientations towards participation in Britain. Chapter Five examines the theoretical implications of technological development, the diversity of the management function, and changes in the social composition of management, to discover management's attitudes towards worker participation, and contrasts this with the results of recently collected data. In the following chapter a number of the themes touched on in earlier chapters are brought together in a consideration of the British experience of worker participation in the boardroom.

A dominant theme in the discussion and practice of worker participation has been its relationship to efficiency. Historically it has been viewed both as a formula for and as a threat to the effective operation of industry. Chapter Seven examines the relationship between workers' participation and the political economy of the work group, the firm, and the society. This theme is continued into the next chapter but with a different focus. A number of companies, communities and societies have introduced a variety of forms of worker ownership into the organisation of their economic systems. The chapter examines financial participation, co-operative ownership and self management systems, and looks at the implications of worker ownership for worker participation. The final chapter draws together a number of the themes of earlier chapters but also goes on to consider whether, in the light of the economic depression of the 1980s, the earlier trend towards increased worker participation is likely to be sustained.

Further Reading

Pateman (1970) provides not only useful definitional material but a short synthesis of a number of other studies; the book also offers an important theoretical bridge between work on political democracy and on industrial democracy; this is further developed in Pateman (1975) and Pateman (1983). Useful general comparative background can be found in Sanderson and Stapenhurst (1979) which covers a wide variety of aspects of economic and worker participation with special emphasis on North America, and in Vanek (1975), Garson (1976) and Garson (1977), Burns et al. (1979) and Crouch and Heller (1983). ILO (1981) presents a relatively up-to-date description of the variety of institutional forms of worker participation which are extant internationally. A more theoretical comparative approach is provided by Sorge (1976), by Marsden (1978) (who usefully illustrates some of the pitfalls of comparing institutions across cultures) and by Poole (1981). A methodologically sophisticated approach to comparative empirical work is presented in IDE (1981).

1 · Some Concepts

This chapter examines the way in which classical sociology has conceptualised the relations between employers and employees, and how these ideas have been developed and modified in the work of more recent sociologists. The chapter is structured around the work of Marx, Durkheim and Weber and their concern with the effects of market, technological and organisational development on social conflict and social integration in industry. Much of the material dealt with in this chapter will be referred to again in later chapters. It is set out here in order to clarify the intellectual development of ideas and to raise a variety of themes in a preliminary but integrated fashion.

Market, technology and alienation: Marx

There are two main, interconnected strands in Marx's work which are relevant to a discussion of participation, relating to the theory of capitalist development and to the alienating effects of the division of labour. According to Marx, every society is based upon a set of relations of production. Under capitalism workers sell their labour power to the capitalist who also buys in other factors of production. Products are no longer produced simply for their 'use value,' that is, because they are needed, but because they have an 'exchange value'—they can be sold. But more than that the capitalist is looking to produce commodities which have a greater value than the value of the labour and materials that went into their production, that is, to create 'surplus value.' 'Since production is only undertaken to increase the value at the disposal of the capitalist, capitalists are compelled constantly to seek out new ways to increase the exploitation of their labour in order to expand their capital at the fastest possible rate.' (Walton and Gamble, 1976, p. 123).

Exploitation may be increased, according to Marx, in two main ways: through 'absolute' or 'relative' extraction. Absolute extraction is producing more output from labour at a given wage either by increasing the pace of work or the hours worked. This is crude and subject to limits — neither speed nor the length of the working day can be increased indefinitely. Relative extraction increases surplus value by increasing productivity through improving the means of production, typically by investing in new technology. Relative extraction has of course been the dominant mode of expansion (p. 124). Technological development also has the effect of increasing the division of labour and turning the worker into a mere 'appendage of the machine.'

While Marx understood capitalism as a powerful mechanism for increasing material wealth, he saw its development as necessarily subject to cyclical crises. These were generated by a number of interconnected elements. As technology expands then fewer workers are needed; a reserve army of labour is created. This acts to keep down the wages of those in employment. In times of boom, however, capital increases production by drawing in reserves of labour power from the pool of labour. But draining the reserve pool of labour has the effect of increasing wages, and diminishing surplus value. The expansion of technology is also related to a trend towards the centralisation and concentration of capital. Individual capitalists expand the amount of capital under their control and there is also at the same time a merging of existing capitals. The effect of both processes is to lead to larger and larger production units. At some point in this cycle the increases in productivity begin to decline and there is also a tendency for the rate of profit to fall. As the rate of profit falls investment declines, part of the labour force has to be laid off, this further diminishes consumer purchasing power and so the spiral continues until wages are forced down to such a level that new conditions exist for the creation of surplus value. During the crisis some of the less efficient entrepreneurs will have gone out of business; those remaining can take their share of the market. Expectations of accumulation improve and a new cycle starts.

The more capitalism develops, and the more productive the economy, the less control the worker is able to exercise over the object that he or she produces. Marx described this process as one of alienation. His conception of alienation comprises a number of elements. First, the worker has no control over the product he produces; his labour power, along with other factors of production, belongs to the capitalist and the commodity he produces is the property of the capitalist. The product of his or her labour becomes an alien object. Second, the worker is alienated from, and in, the productive task itself. Work becomes a means to an end rather than an end in itself. Since labour is forced it cannot be satisfying. Third, since economic relations are also social relations, capitalism reduces human relations to the operation of the market. Finally, given that man is essentially a social being, the character of capitalist society separates man from his essentially human nature (Giddens, 1971, p. 12). Giddens suggests that there are two distinct but related sources of alienation in Marx's analysis, both rooted in the division of labour within capitalist production. He has termed these 'technological alienation' and 'market alienation' respectively. 'The latter expresses the fact that the organisation of production relationships constitutes a class system resting on an exploitative domination of one class by another; the former identifies occupational specialisation as the source of the fragmentation of work into routine and undemanding tasks' (p. 229). For

Marx, both arise out of the division of labour into owners and producers and can only be overcome by the ending of that division.

Some later commentators have agreed with Marx in seeing the development of the labour process under advanced capitalism as increasing the degree of alienation. Braverman, for example, argues that pursuit of profit has led to an increasing deskilling of work; this has two aspects. First, there has been a division of labour, between the conception and the execution of tasks. Second, and as a consequence of the separation of conception and execution, the production process is divided between sites and also between separate bodies of workers.

Braverman cites the scientific management movement and in particular the work of Taylor as central to this process*; the work of the human relations school he sees as its adjunct. 'Work itself is organised according to Taylorian principles while personnel departments and academics have busied themselves with the selection, training, manipulation and pacification and adjustment of "manpower" to suit the work process as organised. Taylorism dominates the world's production; the practitioners of "human relations" and industrial psychology are the maintenance crews for the human machinery.' (Braverman, 1974, p. 87). Capitalism has developed and encouraged these processes because deskilling permits labour power to be bought at lower costs and ensures control over the execution of work. From this perspective, participation is seen as successful management practice, a means of intensifying the process of management control over labour in the production process, and all participation schemes are in both intention and effect pseudo participation.

Braverman has been criticised for being ahistorical and indeed romanticising the position of the pre-capitalist worker, for implying a unilinear and unitary process of the appropriation of control by capital; for neglecting the negative effects of deskilling (active involvement by the worker in work can have positive effects for capital) and for treating workers as passive and ignoring both their subjective and collective responses to industrial developments (Nichols, 1980, p. 272). Whilst writers such as Braverman have seen technological development as decreasing labour control over the production process, other writers have taken a different view. Blumberg has argued that technological development has led to increased alienation amongst the workforce but also to a growing concern to counter this through participative practices in industry. 'The alienating character of much industrial labour, discussed so often since the days of Marx and still of prime importance in our world, seems to be *substantially mitigated* by the introduction of various forms of direct workers'

*F. W. Taylor initiated the systematic study of industrial behaviour at the end of the nineteenth century and his work has had an important and continuing influence since then. His system of scientific management revolves around three elements, organisational structure and routine, the measurement of work and task design, and the selection and motivation of workers (see Rose, 1975, pp. 31-62).

participation. An impressive panoply of research findings demonstrates consistently that satisfaction in work is significantly enhanced by increasing workers' decision-making powers on the job. Under a great variety of work situations and among workers of vastly different levels of skill work satisfaction has been shown to increase even though the technical process of production and the workers' tasks themselves remain unchanged. The cumulative weight of this research is slowly beginning to change the sociologist's image of the worker; to a growing number of writers, the modern worker is perhaps best understood as being orientated and responsive to participation.' (Blumberg, 1968, p. 2).

Other writers have suggested that technology can decrease as well as increase work alienation. Blauner, for example, distinguishes four modes of industrial powerlessness: separation from ownership of the means of production and the finished product, inability to influence general managerial policy, lack of control over conditions of employment, and lack of control over the immediate work process. He argues however that control over conditions of employment and over the immediate work process are the most important for manual workers, who are likely to be unconcerned with control at the managerial or ownership level. 'Unlike the absence of control over the immediate work process "ownership powerlessness" is a constant in modern industry and employees therefore normally do not develop expectations for influence in this area.' (Blauner, 1964, p. 17).

The aspects of alienation which Blauner emphasises are those that are tied to the specifically technological characteristics of industry. He outlines four positions on a technological continuum; craft industry, machine minding, assembly line and process industry; he suggests that alienation will be lowest at either end of the continuum, that is that in the craft and process industry the technology allows the worker to have a greater degree of control over his work, that the work is meaningful, the work group is socially integrated, and as a consequence work does not lead to self-estrangement. He argues that in the long term the increase in process and automated industry will decrease the alienation of the industrial worker (p. 192). In the short run he advocates a variety of job satisfaction techniques such as job rotation and job enlargement as solutions to alienation in mass production industry (p. 184).

Blauner's work has been subject to a variety of methodological and conceptual criticisms (Berg et al, 1978; Eldridge, 1971). From the perspective of this book a number of points should be noted. In concentrating on control over the immediate work situation, and treating the content of control at other levels as a social given, Blauner ignores possible interrelationships between the levels. Moreover, in concentrating on the task level he focuses effectively on task satisfaction and attitudes; attitudinal measurement psychologises the concept of alienation whereas the Marxian concept revolves around social relationships. This is not to say that the relationships between technology and task control are not important, but that it is difficult to move from analysis at that point to making statements about the extent of alienation in industrial society; and that the relationships between technology, organisation size, and wider control implicit in Marx's formulation, are omitted from Blauner's subjective formulation. Nevertheless Blauner's work is important in reversing the Marxian assumption that technological advance necessarily decreases the power and control of the workforce.

A number of French sociologists also see technological development as leading to new pressures towards and possibilities for increasing worker participation in industry. They have suggested that the growth of process technology is creating a 'new working class' whose position in the production process produces both a new consciousness and an ability to exercise control in the workplace (Mallet, 1975; Touraine, 1971). Mallet argued that, while technological development had deskilled work within mass production industries, capitalism, by raising the standards of living of the workforce successfully, had moved their interest away from issues of control in the workplace towards a purely consumer-oriented, instrumental attitude towards work – this he termed '*la lutte pour le beefsteak*.' The development of new technologies, however, creates a new relationship between the worker and the enterprise; highly skilled technical labour is required. Labour becomes a fixed rather than variable cost; it has high paid, stable employment. The worker's life is bound up with the enterprise; but more than that his skill gives him a major degree of power over and knowledge of the enterprise. The worker in the advanced sector can grasp the nature of his own alienation and will be led to overturn the existing relations of production (Mallet, 1969 and 1975).

Gallie has recently criticised the work of both Blauner and Mallet for basing overarching theory on a frail base of data (Gallie, 1978, p. 29). Moreover, there is some confusion in their work between 'core plant' technology, that is, the technology associated with the central production process of the plant, and 'dominant' technology, the most widespread technology in the plant. Associated with that is the confusion of workers manning the core technology with typical workers in the industry. Nichols and Beynon, for example, found that in six out of seven plants of a major chemical company the control room operative, the typical process worker, was in a minority; three quarters of plant workers were engaged in direct manual semi- and unskilled work (Nichols and Beynon, 1977). More importantly however, on the basis of a study of similar automated plants in France and Britain, Gallie has concluded that 'advanced automation proved perfectly compatible with radically dissimilar levels of social integration and fundamentally different institutions of power, and patterns of trade unionism. Instead our evidence indicates the critical importance of wider cultural and social structure patterns of specific societies for determining the nature of social interaction within the advanced sector.' (Gallie, 1978, p. 295).

Other writers have also placed less emphasis on technology and have understood aspects of worker participation, more broadly, as 'attempts to change relationships of production in such a way that they are accommodated to changes in the means of production', thus pointing to 'a tendency amongst human groups to react to tension between the means of production and existing social relations by reorganising these social relations.' (Brannen et al., 1976, p. 246). Within this context changes in technology, in the structure of industry and the nature of markets, in the organisation of management, the State and trade unions, are considered empirically in relation to the distribution of power and control within industry and their effects on its authority structure. Because capitalism develops unevenly and distributes rewards unevenly it generates discontent and opposition. The emergence of discontent, particularly of an organised and powerful kind, through for example a labour movement, leads directly or indirectly to socio-economic policies and institutions designed to regulate or dissipate discontent; welfare and labour legislation, and the development of the institutions of collective bargaining, arbitration and conciliation are examples. Whilst the development of these institutions may limit social conflict, they also create new goals, norms and aspirations and new bases of influence and power from which to press for these.

One of the aspirations and also the mechanisms of conflict regulation which arises is participation. The pressures for this can emerge from the development of a democratic culture, leading to a clear contradiction between the rights of the individual as citizen and his or her subordination in the workplace; it can also be a reaction, within the labour movement, to problems confronted within industry, an attempt by workers to gain greater control over their working lives; and it can be promoted by individual managers or by government, both as a reaction to conflict and also as an attempt to increase worker attachment to the enterprise and commitment to production (Baumgartner et al., 1979). A number of authors have argued that pressure for participation has ebbed and flowed in particular historical periods (Poole, 1978) and that these waves relate to particular points of crisis in the economic system (Brannen et al., 1976). Within this context Ramsay has argued that experiments in participation should be viewed as a management response to crises in industry generated by upsurges in labour power; but participation schemes have not been successful in management terms. Capitalism is seen as both 'engendering and rendering impotent such movements for participation.' (Ramsey, 1977, p. 498). Within this perspective participation reforms are simply cosmetic; they mask, he argues, the alienated character of labour under capitalism.

Social integration and social inequality: Durkheim

Durkheim, like Marx, attempted to understand the implications of the division of labour and of industrialisation within a capitalist society. His central preoccupation was with social integration and how this was achieved. Social integration within industrial society was, however, problematic.

Industrialisation has created a differentiated division of labour and whilst a new form of social integration — which he termed 'organic solidarity', based on the functional interdependence of roles — might be achieved, this had not yet come about. Like Marx he saw society as divided into two broad classes, capital and labour, which were in conflict. Unlike Marx however he did not see this conflict as an inevitable outcome of the division of labour. It arose because the division of labour was incomplete and imperfect.

This incompleteness was for him related to two main pathologies, the anomic division of labour and the forced division of labour. The first of these referred to the lack of development of a set of moral beliefs which was in tune with the conditions of modern society. In part this was related to the lack of connection between consumer and producer, and in part to the lack of connection between worker and finished product which industrialism created. Producers were unable to relate their activities to consumer need, thus problems of over-production and economic crisis were created; workers were unable to relate their activities to the finished product and thus work became boring and degrading and workers themselves passive and unresponsive to the changing needs of the organisation.

The anomic division of labour however was buttressed by the forced division of labour. This meant that the development of a class structure led to the allocation of positions within the division of labour on grounds other than those of merit or ability, and the creation of an artificial and dysfunctional barrier to equality or opportunity. He saw the hereditary transmission of wealth as a very important factor in promoting inequality; and as being inimical to social integration. Giddens has summarised this theme as follows: 'While the functioning of organic solidarity entails the existence of normative rules which regularise the relationships between different occupations this cannot be achieved if these rules are unilaterally imposed by one class on another. These conflicts can be obviated only if the division of labour is coordinated with the distribution of talents and capacities and if the higher occupational positions are not monopolised by a privileged class.' (Giddens, 1971, p. 80). It is important to note however that Durkheim did not see the elimination of the forced division of labour as bringing about the end of anomie; it was simply a necessary condition for this. The absence of regulation spells out moral anarchy no matter who owns the means of production. Class relations can be changed without eliminating anomie; anomie could not be dealt with in a situation of unequal class relations. By contrast Marx saw the end of class relations, that is market relations, as leading to the disappearance of alienation.

Durkheim also argued that occupational activity should be regulated by those involved in that activity. He envisaged occupational associations which would regulate the social organisation of production in each industry. The full development of the organic division of labour would imply that these regulatory groups took over the ownership of the means of production, supplanting the institutions of inherited wealth and private property. These occupational associations are seen as providing a means both for the social integration of the individual and the articulation of the various parts of the industrial system. They also act as important secondary groups, between the individual and the State. Eldridge has pointed out that Durkheim's discussion of the role of occupational associations 'is not so different from G. D. H. Cole's discussion of guild socialism. But there is no attempt as in some versions of syndicalism to supersede the political sphere of rule by the economic.... The need for state intervention in the various fields of collective life is not disputed but in order to check any tyrannical tendencies the secondary groups need to be established. This is the checks and balances principle of democratic rule – so industrial democracy would be envisaged as an integral part of the whole.' (Eldridge, 1982). Others have taken a different view and have perceived Durkheim's analysis as providing a blueprint for various forms of state and industrial corporatism. As Newman points out however, Durkheim, 'with his life long identification with the goals of social democracy would seem an unlikely contender for the role of spiritual leadership in a movement, professedly hindward-looking and moreover stringently authoritarian' (Newman, 1981, p. 8).

Others have seen the work of the human relations school, and of the neo-human relations school with its emphasis on communication and job satisfaction, as related in part to the notion of anomie. (This is further discussed in Chapter Four). However, the emphasis which Durkheim placed on the coordination of a plurality of interests, his stress on the need for the autonomy of worker interest associations, and his awareness of the relationship between industrial conflict and stratification within the wider social system, is different from the unitary, plant-oriented analysis of members of that school. Its prescriptions 'were directed at anomie while leaving intact the power enforced structures of bureaucracy, subordination, and reward which gave rise to it.' (Fox, 1974a, p. 235).

Durkheim's notion of anomie has been utilised in a broader and explicit way to analyse the pattern of British industrial relations. Fox and Flanders argued that whilst the institutions of collective bargaining provided a form of regulative, normative order, there were severe pressures within the system leading to the breakdown of this normative order, that is to a state of anomie (Fox and Flanders, 1969). These derived from the proliferation of norm-creating groups, the high incidence of strikes, chaotic pay differentials and uncontrolled movements of earnings and labour costs, ultimately threatening through inflation the government's ability to govern. Their ideas for the recreation of a normative order were based on an expansion of collective bargaining agreements at the workplace over such things as job evaluation and productivity, and at the industry level over wages and rules governing such issues as careers and discipline. They also stressed the need for an agreed and continuing incomes policy at national level. Their proposals for the reintegration of the normative order depended on the participation of the unions in the decision-making process, through collective bargaining.

However, normative regulation resulting from bargaining is unlikely to rest purely on consensus; as Goldthorpe has pointed out it will be a product of the balance of power between the parties concerned and their calculation of what is the most advantageous position they can achieve at any point in time; or of the imposed intervention and creation of common norms by a third party. To the extent that the normative order is the product of the calculation of advantage under given constraints or is imposed by a third party, it is unlikely to be continuously effective. 'Thus while proposals for reform of the kind that Fox and Flanders put forward might well endow collective bargaining institutions and procedures with a good deal more formal rationality than they at present possess I find it difficult to believe that such measures could go very far towards ensuring *stable* normative systems of either a substantive or a procedural kind at any level of industrial relations.' (Goldthorpe, 1974, p. 225).

Moreover, Goldthorpe argues, the analysis of Fox and Flanders is limited in that it does not follow Durkheim in relating the problem of anomie to that of inequality: 'the existence of inequality, of an extreme, unyielding and largely unlegitimated kind does militate seriously against any stable normative regulation in the economic sphere — because it militates against the possibility of effective value consensus on the distribution of economic and other resources and rewards.' (p. 229). The form of participation through collective bargaining, whilst preserving the union's independence from management, presents no challenge to management's ultimate authority and indeed accepts and underwrites it.

Authority, subordination and efficiency: Weber

Marx was concerned with the economic order and saw the division of labour between the owners of the means of production (and their agents) and the rest of society as central to understanding the relationships of production. Durkheim was concerned with the moral order and the implications of the division of labour within modern society for normative integration. For Weber 'rational calculation is the primary element in modern capitalist enterprise and the rationalisation of social life generally is the most distinct attribute of modern western culture' (Giddens, 1971, p. 241).

Weber saw the division of labour as having a number of technical, social and economic elements. In any society there can be a low or high degree of differentiation of tasks; there can be individual labour or combined labour and a variety of combinations of human and material means of production; there can also be a variety of types of material means of production. Both labour services and the material means of production may be owned by labour itself (individually or collectively) or they may be bought on a contractual basis by entrepreneurs. Where labour owns its own labour services and the material means of production it can carry out the management work itself or hire others to do it. Where entrepreneurs have appropriated the means of production and bought labour services, they will either carry out the management function themselves or appoint agents to do this.

Weber argues that there are a number of technical reasons why within industrial society, the individual worker is expropriated from the means of production. The technology may require the services of many workers at the same time or successively; the rational exploitation of energy sources may mean a large number of tasks have to be carried out simultaneously under unified control; there may be a need to combine complementary processes under common supervision; or to have large scale undertakings run by a coordinating and technically trained management; or there may be a technical need for controlling speed, effort and quality. These factors do not exclude the possibility of the appropriation of the means of production by collectivities of workers, as in a cooperative.

However, there are economic reasons for the expropriation of workers in general, including technical and clerical workers. 'It is generally possible to achieve a higher level of economic rationality if the management has extensive control over the selection and modes of use of workers as compared with a situation created by the appropriation of jobs (by workers) or the existence of rights to participate in management. These latter conditions produce technically irrational obstacles as well as economic irrationalities.' (Weber, 1978, p. 138). He cites the possibility that workers will emphasise job rights and wages and that this will often be 'in conflict with the rationality of organisation'. He argues that the development of industrialisation has favoured the expropriation of labour because it puts a premium on capital accounting, on the purely commercial qualities of management and on speculative business policy; and also because of 'the sheer bargaining superiority which in the labour market any kind of property ownership grants to employers over and against workers' (p. 138).

Weber makes a distinction between 'formal' and 'substantive' rationality. Formal rationality refers to the extent to which it is possible to carry through accurate rational calculation and to act on its results. Within an economic framework 'expression in money terms yields the highest degree of formal calculability' (p. 85). Substantive rationality refers to the fact that social action is not simply based on rational calculation but that other criteria enter into the equation – criteria related to ethical, political, status and other values. Weber sees fundamental elements of tension in the modern economy between formal and substantive rationality. He argues, for example, that the 'fact that the maximum of formal rationality in capital accounting is possible only where the workers are subjected to domination by entrepreneurs is a further specific element of irrationality in the modern economic order' (p. 138). He is also aware that whilst formal rationality suggests that worker ownership and worker participation are not economically efficient, nevertheless 'the appropriation of the means of production and personal control (by workers), however formal, over the process of work constitutes one of the strongest incentives to unlimited willingness to work' (p. 152). Within the capitalist system, by contrast, 'the most immediate bases of willingness to work are opportunities for high piece rate earnings and the danger of dismissal' (p. 151). He also notes that 'though they are formally expropriated it is possible for an association of workers to be in fact in a position to exact for itself an effective share in management or in the selection of management personnel' (p. 137).

The relationship between the spread of formal rationality and the attainment of substantive rationality is problematic. Whilst modern rational capitalism is the most advanced economic system that man has developed, the rationalisation of social life which has made this possible has consequences which contravene other values such as those of individual creativity and autonomy. Weber understood that capitalism entails the formation of a class system based on capital ownership and wage labour. But the central characteristic of capitalism, in his view, is the rationalisation of activity in the division of labour. This is not simply confined to the sphere of industry but applies to many institutional areas. It is the relationships of authority and subordination which are important rather than the relationships of production. Any form of organisation can be subject to expropriation of the means of administration. The socialisation of the means of production is no answer to the problem of bureaucratisation. It would simply increase the extent of bureaucratic administration.

Bureaucratic organisation, that is, organisation based on rational authority, is the characteristic form of social organisation within industrial society. Weber, as we noted earlier, makes a distinction between the notion of power and the notion of authority or domination. Power is simply the probability that one actor within a social relationship will be able to carry out his or her will despite, or over and against others within that relationship. Authority is a particular case of the exercise of power in which a command is obeyed because the subordinate accepts the legitimacy of his superordinate. He distinguishes three types of authority: traditional authority, that is authority based on customary rules; charismatic authority, that is authority based on the extraordinary qualities of an individual; and rational authority, resting on the belief in the legality of patterns of normative rules and the right of those given authority by these rules to issue commands. Those subject to this latter form of authority owe no personal allegiance to a superordinate and follow his commands only within the restrictive sphere in which his jurisdiction is clearly specified.

The pure form of bureaucratic organisation has a number of features; staff perform regular duties, spheres of competence are clearly marked, there is hierarchy of officers in relations of sub- and super-ordination, there are written rules governing conduct, recruitment is based on competence and qualification, and individuals simply fill offices but do not own them. Bureaucratisation is seen by Weber as the necessary pattern of organisation for industrial society. It is not associated with specialisation of functions simply in the economic sphere but in the political, military and other areas of society as well. 'The efficiency of the bureaucratic organisation in the conducting of routinised tasks necessary for a modern economy is the main reason for its spread; indeed it is the only form of organisation which is capable of coping with the immense tasks of coordination necessary to modern capitalism'. (Giddens, 1971, p. 59).

Weber's sociology has not been directly applied or developed to any great degree by scholars interested in issues of worker participation. This is partly owing to its schematic nature, partly to its inaccessibility, and partly also, no doubt, to the inherent pessimism of Weber's view that the trends towards the rationalisation of economic life and towards bureaucratisation were irreversible, 'a cage within which men would be increasingly confined'. (p. 184). Discussion has however centred around a number of issues which are importantly related to participation: issues of bureaucracy, organisational efficiency, authority and power.

A number of writers have suggested that Weber's model of bureaucracy may itself not be totally rational. Merton for example argues that a structure which is rational in Weber's sense may generate a variety of rigidities which are detrimental to the achievement of the organisation's goals (Merton, 1957). Others have pointed out that the exercise of formal authority will often come up against alternative goals held by sub-units in the organisation which may conflict with the purposes of the organisation as a whole. Different management functions such as production and personnel are likely, for example, to place different values on different sources of knowledge. Parsons has pointed out that Weber's emphasis on both professional (knowledge-based) and hierarchical elements of authority may well give rise to conflict of this kind (Parsons, 1947). Gouldner has noted that rules can be interpreted as minimal standards of performance and in order to achieve organisational goals need to be buttressed by additional sanctions or rewards (Gouldner, 1955).

Whilst managers have authority over workers, as Brown points out, the contract of employment is unspecified and necessarily vague in task terms (Brown, 1981). Management needs to bolster its formal authority through the use of other forms of power. For example, various forms of information disclosure can be seen as means of exerting influence, and the threat of redundancy or closure as forms of coercion. The exercise of managerial authority is constantly under challenge through customary practice, through the operation of the unions, and through protection given to the workforce (or extracted by the workforce) from the State. Whilst the workforce has little formal authority it is able to exercise varying degrees of power over management. Both management and workforce possess a variety of power resources. 'The distribution of such resources is not simply an artifact of the distribution of authority, for there are significant differences in the power of groups possessing the same degree of authority, or even in reversal of the distributions of authority.... Moreover the allocation of authority between management and workers is not paralleled by a similar distribution of power: in contemporary capitalism work groups have more power than authority.' (Martin, 1977, p. 125). As Watson has indicated 'every organisation is thus confronted by a basic paradox: the means used by the controlling management of the organisation to achieve whatever goals they choose or are required to pursue in an efficient way (i.e. at the lowest feasible cost short- and long-term) do not necessarily facilitate that efficient achievement of goals, since these means involve human beings who have goals of their own which may not be congruent with those of the people managing them.' (Watson, 1980, p. 196).

Abell argues that this paradox is becoming so strong that 'we are in part witnessing the demise of Max Weber's rational legal form of legitimation and thus in many respects (though not all) of his rational bureaucratic form.' (Abell, 1979, p. 142). He suggests that just as Weber was able to document a decline in the importance of traditional and charismatic authority 'so likewise we can chart the decline in rational legal forms of legitimation' and a tendency towards 'democratic authority structures' (ibid.). He argues that in Weber's ideal type of legal rational authority there is a hierarchical coincidence of the co-ordinating function, necessary to co-ordinate tasks within organisations, with the control function, necessary to ensure that individuals and groups within organisations do not simply pursue their own diverse self-interests. However, insofar as there is a need for control, then there is no reason to suppose it should necessarily follow the structuring principles of co-ordination. Abell suggests that the structuring of the control function might be independently arrived at through the principles of equality, representation, competence, and efficiency (which he terms 'the principles of rational democratic authority'). The latter principle 'may of course determine a certain overlap in control and co-ordinative roles' (p. 164).

Conclusion

The topic of worker participation is about the control of workers, in the sense both of control by them and control exerted on them within the system of production. The relevance of the topic arises from the fact of the division of labour at the level of the economy itself, at that of the task, and at intervening levels; it is concerned with both the causes and the consequences of that division. The purpose of this chapter has been to locate the topic within a broad perspective but also to introduce a range of ways of thinking about worker participation and the factors that have a bearing on it. In subsequent chapters we shall be drawing upon concepts referred to here and looking further at some of the literature mentioned.

Further Reading

Giddens (1971) supplies a useful introduction to the ideas of Marx, Durkheim and Weber. Eldridge (1973) connects a number of classical themes to the work of later industrial sociologists. Watson (1980) and Hill (1981) are helpful and comprehensive introductions to the sociology of industry and of work, which provide a broader context to many of the themes touched on in this book. Fox (1974b) provides a more focused discussion and analysis of the challenges to managerial authority in modern work organisations and of the role of participation. Blumberg (1968) and Poole (1978) provide important links between conceptual issues, particularly those of alienation and of power, and substantive topics in the area of worker participation.

2 · Some History

Issues of participation and industrial democracy are not new. They have been articulated, fought over, conceded and rejected since the earliest years of industrial society. All industrial market societies have in the course of their development suffered strains between the relations and the means of production. These have expressed themselves in different ways and a variety of institutional patterns has evolved in response to them. Sorge has argued that, whilst industrialisation processes produced common problems in western market economies, the solution to these problems has differed because, whilst strains in the industrial relations systems emerged at particular points in time, the particular circumstances prevailing varied. He suggests that the particular industrial patterns which developed in each country in the twentieth century emerged out of their history in the preceding century. In particular he argues that in countries such as Germany in which the state took a repressive stance towards labour, withholding the freedoms of association and combination, it both radicalised the labour movement, involved itself in the conflict between capital and labour, and was essentially forced to introduce legally based forms of worker participation. In countries where association and combination were allowed, such as Britain, voluntary forms of regulation emerged, based on contractual or customary relationships between workers and employers (Sorge, 1976).

This chapter looks at the emergence and development of participatory forms within British society from the early nineteenth century until the period immediately following the second world war. In the next chapter we examine more recent history. These chapters are intended to trace the broad contours of relationships between capital and labour, describe the origins and development of a variety of institutional forms for regulating these relationships, and sketch in the economic and normative context. The British experience should be seen as both unique and common.

The growth of collective organisation
The early decades of the nineteenth century were a time of great turbulence in which the social formations emerging out of the industrial revolution were struggling to define their relationships with each other. They were a time of potent desubordination by the developing working class, in which

many of the themes on which we are still ringing variations were first played.

In the early phase of industrialisation in Britain relationships between workers and owners were based on a 'theory of dependence.' The poor had a duty to be obedient and to carry out without question the tasks set for them by their masters. The masters on their side had a duty to look after their workers and protect them from the vicissitudes of life. In the course of the nineteenth century these values became subordinated to those of the philosophy of self help. Authority was not ascribed but achieved. Wealth or poverty simply reflected differences in effort and ability. The employer's business success was evidence of his hard work and as such justified his absolute authority over the enterprise. But as Bendix has pointed out this assertion of authority only has clearcut meaning as long as the managerial function is in the hands of one man. The idea becomes ambiguous when there is a divorce of ownership from control and the managerial function becomes sub-divided and specialised. It also comes under threat when workers begin to articulate a collective understanding of their position in the work place and to challenge, through the use of collective power, the authority of management (Bendix, 1974).

In 1824, following the repeal of the combination laws which had been passed at the beginning of the century, a plethora of trade societies sprang up; there were some attempts to co-ordinate and organise linkages between them but the financial crash of 1825 checked these activities as industrial unemployment increased and wages dropped. The pick-up in trade at the beginning of the next decade saw a revival of trade unionism and of attempts to co-ordinate the various trades associations at an industrial level, particularly in textiles, pottery and the building industries. The most ambitious scheme was Robert Owen's attempt to form a Grand National Consolidated Union. The policy goal of the union was to organise a general strike of all wage earners throughout the country in order to secure control of the means of production (Redford, 1960, p. 141). Within a few weeks of its formation the Grand National had recruited more than half a million members. However, it found itself encumbered with local and sectional strikes which it could neither co-ordinate nor fund; and the employers and the law made a massive onslaught against it and its trade unions. Attacked on all sides and suffering from internal dissension the Grand National began to collapse in 1834, the same year in which six labourers from Tolpuddle were sentenced and transported to Australia for trade union activities (Pelling, 1971, pp. 39-42).

In the same year another organisation inspired by Owen also collapsed. At the beginning of 1830 there were nearly three hundred co-operative societies in Great Britain. In the next few years the numbers increased to between four and five hundred (Redford, 1960, p. 143 and Thompson, 1980, pp. 871-87). In 1832 the first of a series of exchanges was opened in London for the sale of goods produced on a co-operative basis. The idea was that the goods should be priced according to their 'labour value', that is the amount of labour expended in their production. The exchanges did not work well, partly because the variety of goods produced on a co-operative basis was not large, and partly because some goods were priced high in relation to the open market and remained unsold; and partly because those goods which were better and cheaper than their commercial equivalents were bought up by local tradesmen. By 1834 the exchanges had to be wound up.

Behind much of this activity was an early syndicalist vision in which the exertion of economic power through an integrated trade union movement would be a route to achieving working class control of the State. As one historian reflected, 'When Marx was still in his teens, the battle for the minds of English trade unionists, between a capitalist and socialist political economy, had been (at least temporarily) won.' (Thompson, 1980, p. 912). This vision faded in the defeats of the mid-thirties. In the following twenty years 'the workers returned to the vote as the more practical key to political power.' (p. 913). In the decades of the middle of the nineteenth century 'responsible' trades unionism, collective bargaining and self help replaced the more radical demands of the 1830s. The 1860s and early 1870s saw a boom in manufacturing industry. Trade improved, employment and real wages rose. This led to a strengthening and expansion of trade unionism. 'Trade unionism spread in the wake of these conditions to an unprecedented level of activity. It reached new trades and was intensified in old ones. In some activities, as in coal mining, employers strongly resisted the spread, but in the main trading prospects discouraged anti-union pressures.' (Allen, 1971, p. 141). The main developments were the move away from local artisan associations to regional and national union organisations for particular trades, the formation of a national Trades Union Congress in 1868, and the creation of a parliamentary pressure group. During this period permanent negotiating machinery was established in a number of industries and elsewhere arbitration machinery was set up.

In the same period new forms of economic participation appeared. Between 1865 and 1873 thirty employers introduced profit sharing schemes or various forms of industrial partnership. The schemes were often a mixture of profit sharing and co-partnership: 'workers were free to become co-partners by obtaining shares at a preferential rate, but this was not a necessary condition for participating in the division of company profits above the first ten per cent, which was reserved for shareholders' (Bristow, 1974, p. 266). A number of these schemes were specifically introduced in order to prevent the spread of trade union influence, but even those employers who openly acted from these motives 'found themselves condemned as philanthropists by their colleagues.' (p. 269). The period also saw a brief resurgence of producer co-operatives (see Chapter Eight); but both co-operation and co-partnership withered as the economic boom began to break in the mid 1870s.

The industrial depression of the early 1880s fell most heavily on the unskilled and semi-skilled and on those workers operating in industries where sliding scales fixed to prices determined wages; it led to the development of a different and more militant unionism amongst these non-craft industrial workers. Unions were formed in the gas industry and in the London docks. The successful dock strike of 1889 was the first big victory for unskilled labour: it led to a growth throughout the country of new unions, catering largely for non-skilled workers, with low entrance fees and recruiting on a general basis. Their emphasis was on militancy against employers as a basis for recruitment rather than on friendly society benefits. The traditional craft unions also increased their membership during these years. Between 1889 and 1892 there was a great upsurge of industrial conflict based on pay claims, but also on the rejection of sliding scales and the demand for an eight hour day (Cronin, 1979, p. 50). The early 1890s had produced an economic boom and labour was scarce. Pelling suggests that this was part of the reason for the success of the new unions. 'They seemed suitable only for periods of good trade, when labour was comparatively scarce; given a depression there would be ample supplies of unemployed labour to take the place of any unskilled labour that came out on strike.' (Pelling, 1971, p. 102).

Bristow notes that the surge of new unionism coincided with a renewed increase in profit sharing schemes (Bristow, 1974). In the three years from 1889 to 1892, 88 schemes were begun. One of the most cited of these was in the South Metropolitan Gas Company which had been the first target of the Gas Workers' Union. The profit sharing scheme arose immediately out of a demand by the Union for elements of a closed shop and Sunday overtime pay, although the owner of the company, George Livesey, had been interested in profit sharing ideas for some time. The scheme was introduced with a clause disqualifying strikers from the bonus. 'The immediate necessity for our adopting it,' wrote Livesey later, 'was to retain or to obtain the allegiance of the working men, which was fast passing away in the autumn of 1889 under the influence of the Gas Workers' Union.' (p. 277). The Union, nevertheless, struck; 4,000 provincial blacklegs were brought in, the strike was crushed and acceptance of the profit sharing scheme by the men was part of the terms of settlement; union members were, however, subsequently excluded from the scheme (ibid.).

In 1896 the company appointed three worker directors to its Board. They received their normal wage or salary while on directorial duty, plus a fee for attending meetings. Other gas companies also introduced worker directors. 'The worker directors on the boards of these companies seemed to have functioned in the same way as other directors. No special difficulties seemed to have arisen, but the virtue of these schemes in this respect must be seen against the exceptional background of the companies which had successful co-partnership arrangements, were able to provide a high degree of job security, and at the same time had little labour turnover and faced a low level of militant trade union activity.' (Clarke et al., 1972, p. 143). These schemes continued until the nationalisation of the gas industry in 1948.

Syndicalism and guild socialism

In 1896 the Employers' Federation of Engineering Associations was set up and in 1897/8 the first national lockout in the engineering industry took place. The engineering unions were defeated. In the wake of this and the development of political agitation against the existence of the trade unions, as well as a number of adverse judicial decisions, the trade union movement turned its energies to strengthening its political arm. In the first decade of the twentieth century the TUC associated itself with the Independent Labour Party and the labour movement surged forward in Parliamentary representation. In the election of 1900 it had two representatives in Parliament, but in the 1906 election 29 members of the labour movement were elected, some from the ILP, others having been Lib-Lab candidates. Their political pressure led to the passage of the Trades Disputes Act of 1906, which gave the trade unions immunities from prosecution arising out of strike activity, and the National Insurance Scheme of 1909, which not only provided State cushioning against unemployment but also had the effect of increasing trade union membership. The existing friendly societies and trade unions were made the approved agents for the operation of the state unemployment system. Whilst TUC membership grew by 10 per cent between 1901 and 1910 it rose between 1910 and 1913 by 60 per cent to reach 2,680,000.

The end of the decade saw the economy returning to boom conditions and a rapid rise in price inflation. Meanwhile, however, wages had stayed steady and were under increasing pressure. The economy was slow in reacting to new opportunities in steel, chemicals and electrical engineering. The Empire provided a market for traditional goods and for investment but industry was not competitive in the markets for new goods. Output rose through increased labour input but productivity stagnated. Work measurement techniques began to be used by employers and there was an increase in piece work. There was thus the beginnings of a movement away from a laissez faire market view of labour as a commodity, towards a view of labour as a factor which needed to be managed and motivated (Child, 1969, p. 34). It was also a period of structural transformation, with increases in size of plant and firm, and an increase in semi-skilled occupations. 'The peculiar course of economic growth seems to have generated such a welter of problems and frustrations from 1896 to 1913 that discontent came gradually to focus not on specific evils and localised enemies but on the performance of the entire system' (Cronin, 1979, p. 99).

The years 1910 to 1913 saw a new wave of national and local strikes over wages and working conditions. Whilst Parliamentary representation had achieved some gains for the labour movement there was increasing disenchantment and an oscillation within the movement between ideas related to control through Parliament and others advocating direct workers' control. Perhaps the most influential of these ideas were those of the syndicalists and of the guild socialists. Syndicalist ideas were largely imported from France and America and diffused by means of the journal *The Industrial Syndicalist* launched by Tom Mann in 1910. The central core of syndicalist thinking was that social relations at the point of production were the determining factor in social structure. The workplace and workplace unionism were to be the main agents of social change and the central feature of a reconstructed society. Both the State and society more generally would be subordinated to this rule by producers. The most important feature of syndicalism however was not its doctrine but the impetus it gave to demands for shop floor control (Pribicevic, 1959; see also Cole, 1972).

Under the banner of industrial syndicalism amalgamation committees formed in various industries to agitate for consolidation of sectional or craft societies into one single union for each industry. Syndicalist ideas were behind the foundation of the National Transport Workers' Federation, which included both dockers and seamen. They also lay behind the publication, by the Reform Committee of the South Wales Miners, of the 'Miners Next Step': a set of proposals for an organisation to cover the whole of the extractive industry, whose objective would be 'to fight, gain control of and to then administer that industry' (Coates and Topham, 1968, p. 14). There was also a more general strategy for 'the co-ordination of all industries on a Central Production Board, who with a statistical department to ascertain the needs of the people, will issue its demands on the different departments of industry, leaving to the men themselves to determine under what conditions and how the work should be done. This would mean real democracy in real life, making for real manhood and real womanhood. Any other form of democracy is a delusion and a snare.' (ibid.).

Syndicalism as a force in its own right was short-lived but its indirect effects in promoting workshop leaders and fertilising the embryonic shop stewards' movement were much longer lasting. Guild socialism grew out of a synthesis between the production-oriented goals of the syndicalists and the concentration on the State as the main means of achieving socialist goals which had been articulated within more orthodox socialist traditions. Guild socialists insisted that the rights of the citizen both as producer and as consumer needed to be represented. Whilst producers, organised in guilds, should manage and control individual industries, the State should own the means of production and direct overall economic policy to community needs. The argument against the syndicalists was that they claimed everything for the organised workers, who were to 'oust the capitalist from the control of industry, and enter themselves into complete possession of the means of production and distribution.' The argument against the more orthodox socialists was that they were so immersed in wage struggles, that is issues of distribution, that they neglected the fundamental 'question of production – the problem of giving to the workers responsibility and control, in short freedom to express their personality in the work which is their way of serving the community' (G. D. H. Cole, 1972, p. 37).

The guild socialists, however, leant much more towards syndicalist than collectivist ideas. In Cole's words 'syndicalism is the infirmity of noble minds; collectivism is at best only the sordid dream of a business man with a conscience' (p. 52). More importantly, guild socialists envisaged national guilds as developing out of the activities of the trade unions, who would increasingly challenge managerial prerogative and through encroaching control gradually take over the management of industry. The capitalist owner would then be obliged by the squeeze on his profits to look for State help. Industry would be increasingly nationalised but the bureaucratic nature of nationalisation would further stimulate aspirations for workers' control. This would lead in turn to a guild socialist society (p. 146). Both syndicalism and guild socialism, as sets of ideologies and as guides to practice, had in common a stress on self government in industry and militant unionism as a way towards this. These ideas took hold and grew in a time of economic boom, followed by war. They both reflected and stimulated the growth in the organised power of trade unionism at shopfloor and industrial level.

The first two decades of the twentieth century saw the rapid growth of trade unionism and the wider labour movement, its consolidation at national level both organisationally and in the Parliamentary political sphere, and the strong articulation within it of demands for workers' control. On the employers' side the dominant values of self help and laissez faire economics, and the association of high moral values and the legitimacy of command with commercial success, had begun to weaken. The collective power of labour was increasingly recognised, not as a pathological interference with the natural market system but as a legitimate and inescapable element in the system of industrial production. Employers were coming to terms with trade unionism; collective bargaining was increasingly accepted and the demands of the market were pragmatically modified by both the institutional strength of trade unionism and legal measures to protect trade unions and the unemployed.

The number of conciliation and arbitration boards in existence increased rapidly from 162 in 1905 to 352 in 1913 (Pelling, 1971, p. 143). The period also saw attempts by individual employers to modify industrial conflict in other ways. The years between 1908 and the commencement of the war in 1914 saw a further expansion of profit sharing schemes. In the gas industry 29 companies had adopted financial participation by 1909 and 41 by 1914. In the immediate pre-war years gas company directors claimed that their workers were ignoring agitators, and they attributed lower labour costs and the easy introduction of technological change to the popularity of participation (Bristow, 1974, p. 281).

Excluding the gas industry the average number of financial participation

schemes introduced each year grew slowly but steadily in the first decade of
the century and there was another sudden surge forward between the years
1911 and 1914. Bristow argues that 'regardless of how we judge the ultimate
intentions of the British syndicalists or the effectiveness of the Labour party
in its first decade, the arrival of the labour movement in force at
Westminster and the pre-war increase in industrial strikes both in terms of
the number and the extent of strikes, motivated politicians and employers to
examine positive social and industrial policies.' (p. 282). In 1912, 297 MPs
signed a memorandum to Asquith asking for a Royal Commission to be set
up on co-partnership; at the same time bills were promoted in the House of
Commons for transferring commercial firms into co-partnerships. A
promotional committee for co-partnerships was formed in 1912 to lobby
businessmen and this produced 112 enquiries from firms in the last two
months of that year. Most plans however did not come to fruition. They
were defeated either by the coming of war or the resistance of the trade
unions.

Whitleyism and industrial psychology

The outbreak of war in 1914 took the union movement by surprise. At
national and official level the unions (with the exception of the miners)
agreed to regulations for compulsory arbitration in disputes and the
relaxation of trades practices and constraints on labour mobility. These
regulations, and the increased power of labour in a period of wartime
scarcity, led to a rift between the official union movement and its
membership and saw the emergence, particularly in the engineering
industry, of the influence of shop stewards. Shop stewards had existed in
some unions before the war but largely without power and without
bargaining functions. The first three years of the war saw an upsurge in
workshop bargaining particularly in munitions factories. It also saw the rise
of unofficial committees of shop stewards at district level, linking factories
together. Guild socialist ideas exerted a considerable influence on the aims
of the shop steward movement which was seen as an element of encroaching
workers' control of industry. Despite legislation forbidding them strikes
continued through the war years. In May 1917 one quarter of a million
engineering workers were involved in strikes over the extension of craft
dilution from war work to commercial work. Whilst the strikes were not
successful they led to the cementing of national links within the shop
steward movement and the creation of a national leadership for the Shop
Stewards and Workers' Committee Movement.

In the post-war boom years there continued to be demands for workers'
control. In 1919 the miners demanded radical improvements in wages and
conditions and the nationalisation of the mines so that they could be under
joint State and trade union control. This demand reflected 'the ascendance
of guild socialist thinking (which accepted nationalisation as a step to
industrial democracy provided it embodied a major 'encroachment' by the

trade unions into management) at the expense of the anti-nationalisation philosophy of the syndicalists' (Coates and Topham, 1968, p. 249). A government-initiated commission under Sir John Sankey eventually recommended that the principle of State ownership in the mines be accepted; its recommendation was rejected by the government. Guild socialist ideas were also being actively pursued in this period in the building industry where guilds had been set up, under trade union control, to carry out contracts from a number of local authorities for municipal housing.

The events of 1914 onwards prompted new thinking on industrial control amongst employers and government. In the workplace the authority of some employers had been challenged in real terms by the shop steward movement. Some leading employers were publicly voicing fears that power would be taken from them in their factories. Even Quaker employers such as Seebohm Rowntree were worried about 'the demand of the extremist for a complete recasting of the industrial system' (Child, 1969, p. 45). In 1916 a number of building employers came together with the Building Trades Council to set up a 'Parliament' which should be 'the expression of a desire on the part of the organised employers and operatives to render their full share of service towards the creation of a new and better industrial order' (Coates and Topham, 1968, p. 61). In 1916 also a study undertaken by the Garton foundation analysed the causes of industrial conflict and recommended the establishment of joint employer and employee committees in order to give labour a 'voice in matters directly concerning its special interests, such as rates of pay and conditions of employment' (Child, 1969, p. 45).

Partly in response to this report the Government set up a committee under J. H. Whitley, with employer and trade union representatives, to consider relations between employers and employed. 'The idea was that the popular demand for workers' control might be met if such committees, constituted in each industry at national, local and even workshop level were to discuss not only wages and conditions but also problems of industrial efficiency and management' (Pelling, 1971, p. 160). The Whitley Committee originally proposed that there should be joint councils of workers and employers in each industry at national, district and works level. The councils would be autonomous bodies and whilst government help was available the government left the employers' associations and the trade unions concerned to adapt the scheme to their own preferences and requirements. Whilst both British employers and government were determined to resist workers' control they paid considerable lip service in this period to the idea of worker participation. Whitleyism was the officially sponsored compromise with demands for workers' control. The then Ministry of Labour announced: 'such a plan is typically British; it does not make for revolution' (Child, 1969, p. 45).

Between January 1918 and the end of 1921, 73 joint industrial Councils were set up at national level and 33 interim committees which were intended to lead to joint Councils. At local level between 1917 and 1922 more than 1,000 works committees were formed (Flanders, 1968). No committees however were established in mining, in the cotton industry, or in engineering where trade unionism was strong and well established and where the unions already had a high degree of workplace control. Moreover, 'the Federation of British Industries, while admitting in 1919 that workers had genuine grievances, listed the technical disadvantages of any encroachment on managerial functions. It concluded that commercial management should be staffed by those possessing the requisite qualifications and that it could not be subject to any control by manual workers...in short Whitleyism might lead to idealistic professions of a new and joint spirit of service in industry but for all save the most exceptional employers it was not going to mean any reduction in their authority.' (Child, 1969, p. 49).

By 1922 the boom had collapsed. Unemployment had reached beyond two million of the insured population. The slump destroyed the producers' guilds and saw the end of the demands for workers' control and industrial self-government. The power of labour went into rapid decline. The relaxation of pressure on employers gave them a choice between continuing the experiments with new forms of worker participation or reverting back to the older ways. The evidence points in the latter direction. Most of the works committees set up under the impetus of Whitleyism had ceased to function by 1925 and those that were still working had little relationship with the District or National Whitley Councils (Flanders, 1968). Child argues: 'that the initiative for breakdown generally came from the employers' side is sharply suggested by the fact that in the first place the majority of requests for the establishment of works committees had come from workers and not employers.' (Child, 1969, p. 48). There was also a rapid decline in the National Whitley Committees; by 1932 only 51 joint Industrial Councils remained of which 20 had District Committees associated with them; of these Committees some were meeting irregularly and most had reduced their activities to the regulation of wages and conditions (Flanders, 1968). It was only in parts of the public sector, where central or local government was the employer, that Whitleyism continued as an active institution (see Parris, 1973). Another indication of a change in the attitudes of employers is given by the figures for membership of the Welfare Workers' Institute (which was the forerunner of the Institute of Personnel Management); membership in 1919 stood at 700 companies; this had dropped to 250 companies by 1921 (Child, 1969).

Although by 1922 the wave of interest in Whitleyism had disappeared, one other development which sprang from the experience of the war years and the years immediately preceding it was more enduring. The war effort had drawn attention to the importance of the health and physical working conditions of employees for efficiency and productivity. British industrial psychology began to develop an interest in such issues as fatigue, monotony, pace of work and working environment. The founding of the Industrial Fatigue Research Board in 1918 and of the National Institute of Industrial Psychology in 1921 were key elements in this development.* Managers and management thinkers began to pay attention to methods of exploiting those factors which lay within their control, in order to motivate the workforce. Techniques such as work study and other elements of scientific management began to spread. The wider issues of worker participation were put aside. As Child puts it, 'the nature of the new management techniques not only militated against any direct industrial democracy, but in fact implied the assumption of even more control by managers over matters previously left to the "rule of thumb" of the craft workers.' (p. 111). In conjunction with these shifts of emphasis the idea of an equal partnership with labour was 'slowly transformed into the conception of a relationship in which an expert management played the dominant role' (p. 71).

Profit sharing had also re-emerged between the end of the war and the beginning of the recession; it did not have the same wide appeal as it had in the pre-war years, in part at least because owners and managers who aggressively sought to promote enterprise consciousness and efficiency might well turn for guidance to the new discipline of management science, which prescribed industrial betterment, the use of efficiency and personnel experts, and joint consultation (Bristow, 1974, p. 286). Of the evolution and development of profit sharing in the period up to 1920 Bristow concludes that despite the mixed motives of employers who were interested in such schemes the policy was broadly discredited by the pattern of its dissemination. Employers repeatedly showed most interest during periods of intense industrial conflict and union organisation, when rhetoric about the natural community of interests was bound to seem particularly self-serving (p. 263).

The rise and fall of joint consultation

For most of the inter-war years the trade unions were in retreat. Membership declined and, with it, bargaining power. With the defeat of the labour movement in the 1926 General Strike and increasingly widespread unemployment the remnants of the shop stewards' movement collapsed. This is not to say that shop stewards disappeared but that in the inter-war years 'they found it politic to maintain a low profile' (Clegg, 1980, p. 23). The official trade union movement focused its activity on defending nationally negotiated terms and conditions against reductions. As Child has noted, this emphasis on wider institutionalised procedures required at least *de facto* recognition of management authority (Child, 1968, p. 71). The re-armament programme in the period immediately before the second world war brought renewed prosperity to the engineering industry and to

*For a discussion of the work of these institutions in the inter-war years, their relationship to Taylorism, of which they were critical, and their contribution to management thinking see Rose, 1975.

related industries. With economic prosperity there came a resurgence of the shop stewards' movement.

The exigencies of the war effort and the shortage of manpower led both government and employers to look for changes in work practices and a dilution of craft skills, as they had done during the first world war. In 1940 a number of joint management-union production committees began to spring up in individual plants, with government encouragement. Whilst there was initial resistence within the shop stewards' movement, nevertheless, within a year a national conference of shop stewards carried a proposal urging 'the formation of Joint Production Committees in every factory with the fullest facilities for the shop stewards taking full part and accepting joint responsibility for seeing plans are discussed with all the workers and then carried out.' (Coates and Topham, 1968, p. 167). The demand for Joint Production Committees grew in the trade union movement, particularly in engineering. The Engineering Employers responded by agreeing that its members, if they wished, could create works committees with shop stewards. Early in 1942 the government made an agreement with the unions for joint production and consultative committees to be set up in all factories operated by the Ministry of Supply. By the spring of that year the Engineering Employers and the unions had made provision for Joint Productivity, Consultative and Advisory Committees to be set up in all their federated firms. It has been estimated that by the middle of 1943 there were over 4,000 Joint Production Committees operating in private firms in engineering and allied industries, covering some 2½ million workers. In addition there were similar bodies in mining, construction and many other industries.

Nevertheless, in the years immediately following the war there was an immediate decline. By 1948 the number of Joint Production Committees had dropped to only 550 (Clegg and Chester, 1954). Ramsay argues that the main reason for this was worker disillusion with the way in which the committees had been used chiefly to bolster management power, as disciplinary bodies and the like. This is unlikely to be the whole story. The war-time Joint Production Committees had been launched by the unions, supported by the government, with management following reluctantly behind. The indifference of British management to, and ignorance of, good management practice 'led to direct governmental action enforcing the appointment of personnel officers in all but small factories and the compulsory provision of minimum welfare amenities. Shortly after, the government strongly encouraged the widespread establishment of Joint Production Committees following the Essential Work Orders 1941' (Child, 1969, p. 111). Child argues that the whole process of 'admonition from the State was a stigma on British management. As the war proceeded, a number of publications fanned the flames of criticism by the indictment of managerial inefficiencies, and by reporting how hostile managers frequently were to new methods of accommodation with labour.' (ibid.). Indeed, the decline of Joint Production Committees was not welcomed either by the government or the trade union movement.

In January 1947 the proposal for a campaign to revive Joint Production Committees was brought before the National Joint Advisory Council. 'After full consideration the Council agreed to recommend to employers' organisations and trade unions the setting up of joint consultative machinery where it did not already exist, for the regular exchange of views between employers and workers on production questions...' It also agreed that government would actively promote and monitor progress. (HMSO, 1950). The TUC was also in favour of Joint Production Committees: in 1944 the General Council brought out its Interim Report on Post War Reconstruction, which argued that consultation should be kept as a permanent feature of industrial organisation and that works councils should be generally established. The document thought that the setting up of works councils could most easily be done in the public sector because 'in socialised industries there would of course be no difficulty in ensuring that such works councils were set up and consulted' (quoted in Clegg, 1979, p. 134).

Apart from the enthusiasm of both the government and the trade union movement for the reinvigoration of joint consultation in industry, it has been argued by both Clegg and Ramsey that management were also keen to foster joint consultation. Both authors see this management enthusiasm as stemming from the influence that the human relations views of Elton Mayo and his followers were having on British management thinking (Clegg, 1979; Ramsey, 1977). Certainly human relations philosophy was having some impact. A leading management speaker, for example, at the Oxford Management Conference in 1944 said, 'Industrial relations are primarily a matter of psychology. They must be an integral part of all management, not a segregated function. And the key to them is effective leadership at all levels.' (quoted in Child, 1969, p. 116).

There are, however, some reasons for doubting whether the generality of British management were won over to joint consultation because of the influence of human relations philosophy. Most British managers in the immediate post war period were not in touch with or much influenced by management thinking of any kind. The British Institute of Management estimated in 1948 that there were 400,000 practising managers in manufacturing industry alone in Great Britain but that in all of the management institutions there were only 20,000 members (p. 111). Moreover, human relations philosophy was largely antipathetic towards formal consultative processes. Whilst leadership and downward communication were emphasised by the human relations movement, 'it was felt that communication should be informal and via the medium of supervisory leadership rather than channelled through joint consultation. For this last procedure was thought to involve considerable problems of reporting back while the presence of trade unionists as employee representatives might carry the risk of "distorted" information passing back to the shop floor.' (p. 119).

With or without management support, the initiatives taken in 1948 'probably led to the further creation of formal consultative bodies in many sectors and ensured that much of what machinery already operated continued in existence.' (Hawes and Brookes, 1980, p. 355). A survey carried out by the National Institute of Industrial Psychology at the end of the 1940s found that of 751 firms in the sample, 545 (73%) had some form of joint consultation (NIIP, 1952). Another survey covering 598 firms found that within engineering 92% of the firms in the sample had joint consultation and overall 73% of firms said that they had joint consultative committees (Brown and Howell-Everson, 1950). From 1951, however, with the passing of the immediate post war economic crisis, joint consultation went into a rapid decline. In 1957 an unpublished enquiry by the Ministry of Labour suggested that only about one-third of plants with over 500 employees had some form of permanent consultative machinery. In federated engineering establishments the numbers of joint production committees fell by one-third between 1955 and 1961 (Marsh and Coker, 1963). Ramsay suggests that 'the co-operative spirit of the war could not be recreated nor could a genuine transfer of decision making power to workers be achieved through a weak system of advisory committees.' (Ramsay, 1977, p. 492). As the economic performance of industry began to improve 'workers' participation faded from the agenda of both unions and employers. The pressure was off management once more as industry was able for the time being to produce the goods.' (p. 493).

Conclusion

Participation in industry and the legitimacy of the authority of owners and managers have arisen as important issues at frequent intervals and in various ways in the course of Britain's industrial development. Labour's challenges to management have taken a number of forms, the first being a denial of the legitimacy of the principles of ownership and control embodied within capitalism. This was the position of the Owenite movements of the 1830s and of the syndicalist and guild socialist movements eighty years later. Second, was a challenge to the degree of authority exercised by management but not to the right to exercise it. This manifested itself both in the attempt by labour to organise itself, and collectively to resist and modify the exercise of authority by individual owners; and in the exercise of political methods in order to persuade the State to grant both rights and status to organised labour.

There have been two different thrusts within the latter challenge; one questioning managerial rights to decide in the sphere of production, the other distributionalist, with the aim of enhancing the wages and conditions of labour, that is, altering the allocation between wages and profits. The former can be seen in the trade unions' stance on Whitleyism and Joint Production Committees; the latter, traditional collective bargaining, as being the dominant mode of behaviour in the middle years of the nineteenth century and the interwar years. It can also be seen as dominant in the period we shall come to next, that following the second world war.

Challenges to management control have taken place in waves in the periods 1939-50, 1910-20, the 1890s, 1870, 1830s. These periods have been ones of economic expansion following depression; they have been characterised by labour scarcity, and by rising confidence amongst the working classes. They have seen the rapid growth of union membership and rising militancy indicated by waves of strikes. Cronin has argued that both strike waves and unionisation are 'reflections of a broader learning process on the part of workers, stimulated by the effects of different phases of economic development; a common diagnosis rooted in economic change informs conflict and organisation and affects both the desire and the ability of workers to create collective action.' (Cronin, 1979, p. 40). This is not to deny that in intervening periods there had been some advances of organisation within trade unions: but the sudden surge forward has occurred at particular times. Management interest in participation has tended to be reactive; that is it has come forward with participative schemes of increased militancy, when labour was in a strong bargaining position, or it has reacted to pressure for more worker participation from the labour movement and the State.

When the market situation of labour strengthens and the balance of power changes in its favour, participation becomes important as an attempt to come to terms with this. Demands are made by labour in relation both to ownership and control and to the exercise of managerial authority; some accommodation to these demands is made by the state and some interest in participation is expressed by some sectors of management. When their market position weakens workers' demands revert back to distributionalist issues, the State withdraws and management reasserts its authority and control.

But the cycle does not end where it began. Firstly there is an ever increasing richness and awareness of a variety of ways of modifying relationships. Second, institutional mechanisms and awareness of these do not totally die away. The Owenite ideas of co-operative production revived in a modified form in the mid-1860s and again in the twentieth century, though always on the fringes and out of the mainstream of the production process. The early industrial collectivist ideas of the 1830s re-emerged in the syndicalist movement of 1910-20. The financial share ownership schemes of the 1860s continue to reappear. Ramsey notes that in a 1948 survey of firms 29% had profit sharing (Ramsey, 1977). A survey of the British economy in 1950 would have shown some co-ops, some Whitley Councils, some Joint Consultation Committees, some profit sharing, some nationalisation, some enterprises with strong shop steward workshop control, and so on. Whilst there are ebbs and flows, the general process is more akin to a ratchet effect: the fall back after the surge always stops at a higher level than before.

Further Reading
Thompson (1980) supplies an invaluable guide to developments up to the early nineteenth century. Pelling (1971) is a useful account of trade union development throughout the nineteenth and twentieth centuries. Coates and Topham (1968), subsequently republished in 1970 under the title *Worker Control,* is a helpful, if selective, compendium of contemporaneous documents. Clegg (1980) provides an important source of material on industrial relations institutions. Child (1969) offers an excellent account of the development of management thinking in its historical context; see also Bendix (1974). Cronin (1979 and 1980), Poole (1982), Ramsay (1977 and 1983) and Hill (1980) present material relevant to the theme of cycles of conflict and participation.

3 · More Recent Developments

In the period following the second world war, and especially since the 1960s, a number of writers have argued that an important change has been taking place in the relationships between employers and employees in society; this change is described in various ways but generally relates to notions of democratisation in industry and increased worker participation. One commentator writing in the middle of the 1970s argued that 'The current impulsion being given to this long-standing but largely unrealised aspiration promises to transform the industrial system as no other movement has done since the industrial revolution, whilst its effects will be quite as radical and probably more permanent.' (Levinson, 1974). Writing from a different perspective and about Britain only Milliband labelled these processes of change 'desubordination'. He meant by this that people in subordinate positions in the work situation 'do what they can to mitigate, resist and transform the conditions of their subordination'. (Milliband 1978, p. 402). Whilst desubordination is, he argued, an old phenomenon it is 'a much more accentuated and generalised feature of life in Britain now than at any time since the first decades of the last century; and even though it is not a unilinear process and may be less acute in some years than in others, it is more likely to grow than to diminish.' (ibid.).

The formal and informal challenges to authority indicated by Milliband and the development of interest in worker participation are, as we have seen in the last chapter, interconnected. The immediate post-war decades produced an increase in wealth and important improvements in most people's daily lives. These developments did not proceed without imposing considerable strain on the social and economic system. The challenges to authority and the upsurge of interest in a variety of mechanisms of worker participation might be seen as responses to that strain. In this chapter we map out in broad terms the socio-economic context of change. We then look at the way in which the system of labour relations has developed and the implications for worker participation. In particular we consider, alongside the more well known developments, the re-emergence of joint consultation.

Economic change
The period between 1945 and the late 1960s has generally been characterised as one of growth, expansion and industrial development.

'Britain's economic performance since world war two outstrips any earlier period in the past half century' wrote a commentator from the Brookings Institution in 1968 (Caves 1968). Though in comparison with other developed market economies the performance was inadequate, measured by Britain's own economic history the period was one of success, and this was the way it was perceived by those working in the economy. The post-war economic growth led to an expansion of industries in which new techniques predominated, notably electronics, aircraft and motor production, mechanical engineering, new branches of machinery construction, and the petro-chemical industry, all of which took an increasing share of national output and employment. Conversely there was a decline in the relative importance of traditional industries such as textiles, shipbuilding and the manufacture of railway equipment and electrical machinery (Wragg and Robertson, 1978). The period also saw a pronounced trend in industrial concentration in the UK brought about through mergers and acquisitions (including nationalisation), the natural growth of firms and the internationalisation of capital as reflected in the rise of multi-national companies. The rise in the share of production of the hundred largest enterprises has been estimated as being 15% of net output in 1909, 42% in 1968 and about 50% by the mid-70s (Prais, 1976). During the 1960s 45 of the top 120 UK companies lost their independent existence through the process of mergers and takeovers. The merger wave built up to a peak in the early 70s with over 800 acquisitions in 1971 and over 1,200 in 1973. The subsequent years have shown a rapid decline, with just over 500 acquisitions in 1979 (Millward and McQueeney, 1981). Increasingly noticeable, although to a great extent under-researched, has been the growing role of foreign owned multi-national companies in the economy. One report has estimated that by 1976 16% of all enterprises employing over 2000 employees were controlled from overseas (Bullock, 1977, Table 1).

These changes in the industrial structure were mirrored by changes in that of employment and occupations. In 1911 manual workers comprised almost 80% of the working population; by 1971 they made up only 50%. The numbers of self-employed declined considerably as also did the numbers of employers of labour during the same period. By contrast the white collar occupations (clerical, supervisory, technical, professional and managerial), multiplied: in 1911 they accounted for 13.4% of the working population, increasing to 43.3% by 1971, and almost 50% by 1982. The most rapid growth within the white collar sector has been in the areas of scientific, professional and technical work.

The sex composition of the labour force also changed during the post-war period. The rate of participation of women doubled between 1951 and 1971 and there was a very sharp rise between 1971 and 1976, so that in 1976 almost 39% of the labour force were women and almost 50% of married women were working. The industrial distribution of the labour force also changed, with a decline in the numbers employed in traditional industries such as coal mining, shipbuilding, textiles, clothing manufacture and iron and steel, and an increase in employment in chemicals, electrical and mechanical engineering, professional and scientific services and public administration.

The industrial expansion following the second world war required provision of an infrastructure, the cost of which was largely borne by the State. Public expenditure in the United Kingdom as a proportion of GNP rose from 13% before 1914 to 27% after the first world war. By 1951 it had risen to 41%; during the next decade it declined slightly but had returned to that level by 1964. Subsequently it rose steadily to 51.2% in 1968 and 56.2% in 1974. The State also played a direct role in industry through public ownership, the support of firms through the purchase of share capital, direct loans and subsidies, as well as through statutory regulation of a number of aspects of the social and economic organisation of industry. More broadly the post war period saw the emergence of the Welfare State; that is 'a state commitment of some degree which modifies the play of market forces in order to ensure a minimum real income for all. By implication, if not explicitly, this is done to protect individuals against the hazards of incapacity for work arising through sickness, old age and unemployment. There is also general agreement that the objectives of the Welfare State will include a guarantee of treatment and benefit for sickness and injury, and the provision of education.' (Wedderburn, 1965).

Two further characteristics of the post-war period need to be noted. Until the late 1960s the level of unemployment remained relatively low. In 1956, for example, the level of unemployment stood at 1.2% of the working population; in July 1966 it was 1.1%; subsequently it gradually crept upwards, fluctuating around 2.5% during the late 60s and moving rapidly upwards in the early 1970s. Second, the changing occupational structure of the labour force necessitated an expansion in education of all kinds in the post-war period. As the relative demand for manual workers declined the requirement for those with higher educational qualifications increased. The number of first degree graduates rose from a figure of under 10,000 a year in the immediate post-war situation to 82,000 a year by 1976. By the mid-60s 28% of children were leaving school with at least one 'O' level, by the mid-70s around 40%.

The expansion of education and of expectation related to this was part of a wider pattern of rising expectations. In the post-war period large numbers of the working class achieved great advances in their standards of living. Real wages rose and with them the ability to acquire a larger range of consumer goods and an enhanced life style. The expectation of a continually increasing standard of living became part of the value system. This is not to say that each individual or every group had such expectations, nor that the goal was interpreted in the same way by all individuals and groups. What is true, however, is that the expectation of a continuous increase in living standards became a legitimate one for a large part of the working population.

Moreover changes in the industrial and occupational structure, allied with a period of high employment, led to many changes in traditional occupational patterns, widened the range of job choice and job experience and in doing so expanded the range of reference for many occupational groups. Workers' orbits of comparison in job choice, and their criteria against which to judge the relative advantages and deprivations of particular jobs, expanded. Brown argues that this widening of expectations arose partly from discussion in the media of the relative economic performance of Britain and other European countries, partly because public discussion of incomes policies made explicit both what others earned and the question of the criteria which should determine incomes, partly because increasing inflation disturbed a pattern of relative earnings which might otherwise have remained unquestioned, and partly because some of the measures designed to 'rationalise and modernise industrial relations in particular enterprises or industries had the unintended consequence of enlarging the horizons of pay comparisons and disturbing traditional and previously accepted differentials' (Brown, 1978, p. 444).

Institutional responses

The number of unions declined in the post-war period as mergers and amalgamations took place. The growth of new unions seems to have been restricted to the creation of staff and professional associations in the white collar area, particularly during the early 1970s. Trade union membership between 1948 and 1968 grew only gradually and density of membership (that is, actual as against potential membership) dropped slowly until 1968 and then began to rise again. Significantly, the increase in density began to occur at a time when cracks were appearing in the post-war boom and when militancy as measured by the incidence of strikes and the number of working days lost was on the increase.

Whilst in the post-war period there was a general upward trend in strikes, if mining is excluded, there was a fairly stable and low level of stoppages until the late 1950s. The number of non-mining stoppages increased over the period of the sixties, although the number of working days lost remained at a relatively low level (Smith et al, 1978); this was because the 'typical' strike was short, sharp and unofficial. From the late 1960s, however, there was a dramatic increase in both numbers of strikes and numbers of strikers; industrial conflict as measured by stoppages remained at a high level for most of the 1970s.

During the 1960s there was great public disquiet about strikes, related to the fact that a very high proportion of them were 'unofficial.' Flanders saw the number of unofficial strikes as directly related to the growth of plant level bargaining. 'Increasingly over the post-war years national negotiations have been supplemented by bargaining between management and shop stewards inside the plant, the results of which are hardly ever expressed in written agreements.' (Flanders, 1968, p. 18). He lamented the fact that the formal trade union structure had little control over bargaining, which tended to be *ad hoc* and fragmented. However, he also noted that apart from its importance in determining take home pay plant bargaining was 'extending the subjects of collective bargaining beyond the range covered by national agreements. Issues which it would be impossible to regulate uniformly throughout an industry, or on which employers refused to negotiate at national level (such as control of overtime, discipline, redundancy, manning, promotion and working conditions) are no longer being settled unilaterally by management.' (p. 81).

The post-war growth in workplace level bargaining was associated with an increase in the number of shop stewards. The re-emergence of the shop steward in the years immediately preceding the second world war established a permanent trend which was to continue after the war. Shop stewards spread from their base in engineering across other industries and across the public and private sectors. Some shop stewards were accredited by their unions; others were not but were recognised as shop stewards by their employers and treated as such. The Donovan Commission in the mid-sixties estimated a figure of 175,000 shop stewards; it was suggested that this was a 14% increase since the mid-1950s. In 1973 a study carried out by the CIR suggested that there was well in excess of 250,000, though the CIR used a wider definition than Donovan (CIR, 1973). Clegg estimates that using CIR definitions there were over 300,000 shop stewards by the late 1970s of whom 10,000 or more were full-time. This produces more full-time shop stewards than full-time trade union officials (Clegg, 1980).

The post-war period of stable expansion and technological development, rising living standards and widening expectations produced a strong and self-confident trade union movement whose power was most clearly reflected in the expansion of both the amount and scope of bargaining, particularly at the workplace level. Paradoxically the same process of economic development was leading to greater industrial concentration and a shift of management power in the opposite direction. Shop stewards were increasingly seen as the central problem of British industrial relations, responsible for unofficial strikes, forcing wage drift, and re-enforcing restrictive practices. The system of industrial relations was defined as being in a state of disorder, with the informal system of workplace bargaining over piece rates and custom and practice controls over work organisation leading to the undermining of the formal system of industrial relations and the regulation of this formal system by management and trade unions (Fox and Flanders, 1969).

The Labour government set up a Royal Commission under Lord Donovan in 1965 to investigate these issues. It reported in 1968. The solution advocated by the Donovan Commission lay in a re-assertion of both managerial and trade union authority, and the recognition that the regulation of both work and payment systems within the enterprise was important and should be established through effective collective bargaining procedures and the joint regulation of pay and working practices. The Donovan report and analysis was only partly accepted by the government that set up the Commission. Donovan saw little role for the State in the industrial relations area, other than as the provider of an enabling context within which the voluntaristic arrangements between employers and unions could be negotiated. However, from the middle of the sixties State involvement in industrial relations grew.

The period of the late 1960s saw the steady deterioration of the economies of most western industrial countries and the end of the post-war boom. Since 1945 governments in the United Kingdom had generally set themselves four basic economic objectives; full employment, economic growth, a balance of trade surplus and price stability. In most of the early post-war years some, though not all, of these objectives were met. By the late sixties it was beginning to be a struggle to meet any of them. Unemployment began to rise, moving from 2.4% in 1969 to 5% and still rising by 1976; prices began to rise, with Britain's inflation rate persistently above the average of other OECD countries; and economic growth began to stagnate (Caves and Krause, 1980, p. 4). For the first time a new generation of post-war earners saw a threat to their expectations of a continually rising standard of living. The increase in the strike rate was one response to that.

At governmental level there was also a response. The Labour administration produced the White Paper 'In Place of Strife' and made plans to legislate. The legislation was intended to restrict the unions by giving to the Secretary of State powers to enforce a conciliation clause in unconstitutional strikes and other stoppages where adequate joint discussion had not taken place; by enforcing a compulsory ballot in certain serious strikes; and by allowing the government to enforce settlement in inter-union disputes when voluntary conciliations had failed. While the Labour Government dropped its plan to legislate, in the face of trade union opposition, the new Conservative administration which came to power in 1970 brought in the 1971 Industrial Relations Act and followed this in 1972 with a statutory prices and incomes policy. The 1971 Act was intended to control the way unions ran their own affairs, kept agreements and staged strikes. It also outlawed the enforcement of a closed shop. At the same time it granted new protections against unfair dismissal and helped unions to gain recognition with employers.

The return of a Labour Government in 1974 saw a temporary phase of non-interference in the industrial relations area, followed in 1975 by both a prices and incomes policy and legislation which formally set out to strengthen the position of the unions. In opposition the Labour party had come to an understanding with the unions known eventually as the 'Social Contract'; this committed the Labour Government to a programme of measures in industrial relations and in the social and economic sphere in return for co-operation from the TUC in tackling the country's economic problems. As part of the Social Contract the 1971 Industrial Relations Act was repealed and the law on the status and regulation of trade unions was redefined and tidied up. In 1975 legislation was introduced in the field of individual and collective rights and health and safety.

Whilst government attempts to regulate wages through incomes policy met with only short term success and legislation to curb union power was either blocked or subsequently repealed, legal provision expanding individual and collective rights in employment built up from the middle of the sixties. Legislation related to contract of employment limited employers' ability to dismiss workers at will (Contracts of Employment Act, 1963 and 1972) and gave employees a right to compensation if their job should disappear (Redundancy Payments Act, 1965). Workers were also protected against unfair dismissal (Industrial Relations Act, 1971, Employment Protection Act, 1975 (consolidated 1978), amended by 1980 Employment Act) and against discrimination at work on grounds of race (Race Relations Act, 1968 and 1976) and sex (Equal Pay Act, 1970, Sex Discrimination Act, 1975).

Unions were also given collective rights over and against employers. The Employment Protection Act allowed the union to obtain an enforceable award against an employer in a dispute over recognition (this was repealed in 1980), and mandated employers to disclose information to a trade union at their request for purposes of collective bargaining (other than information which might be harmful to an employer's undertaking), and to consult with the unions about dismissal of employees 90 days before if over 100 were to be made redundant and at least 30 days in advance if between 10 and 99 were to be dismissed. Employers had also to consult the trade unions about company pension schemes (Social Security Pensions Act, 1978). The Health and Safety at Work Act (regulations 1977) allowed trade unions to appoint safety representatives in each workplace to carry out inspections; it required employers to consult these representatives in developing measures to ensure health and safety at work and to establish safety committees if necessary. Employers were required to provide time off and relevant facilities to shop stewards and other union officials in connection with their trade union duties (Employment Protection Consolidation Act, 1978).

Voluntarism, intervention and participation
The period following the second world war undoubtedly saw a growth in shop floor bargaining power, albeit localised, sectionalised and confined generally to narrow economistic issues. Its use was largely negative and defensive and seen as frustrating to the economic objectives of management and government. Hence by the early sixties the industrial relations system, based on collective bargaining. was seen to be in crisis. The solution as articulated in the Donovan analysis was to strengthen collective bargaining by formalising procedures, thus maintaining both voluntarism and the independence of the trade union movement. The Donovan analysis was based on a pluralist view of industrial relations. Within such a view the

enterprise is seen as a coalition of individuals and groups with their own aspirations and interests and with widely varying priorities. The individuals and groups however agree to collaborate in a way which allows all participants to get something of what they want. 'The terms of collaboration are settled by bargaining. Management is seen as making its decisions within a complex set of constraints which include employees, consumers, buyers, government, the law, the local community and sources of finance.' (Fox, 1973).

Within this tradition collective bargaining is defined as the major instrument for achieving industrial democracy. Hugh Clegg, writing at the end of the 1950s, had set out the theoretical underpinning of this approach which also reflected the *de facto* position of the leadership of the trade union movement at that time (Clegg, 1960). Clegg argued that independent trade unions are the bulwark of industrial pluralism and that this in turn is the essential component of industrial democracy. The central function of trade unions is to represent and defend the interests of their members. He argued that for several reasons trade unions should never attempt to share the job of management with management itself. He was sceptical as to the technical ability of trade unions to administer industry. Most importantly, he argued that industrial democracy would be destroyed if the trade unions became involved in management. Industrial democracy is created by the existence of an opposition trade union movement. If the trade unions were to participate in management they would be drawn into a conflict of roles, they would have to take on responsibility for management policy and this would undermine their oppositional role.

Blumberg has argued that Clegg's position is both logically and empirically weak (Blumberg, 1968). Opposition in his view is neither a necessary nor a sufficient condition of democracy. To define democracy exclusively in terms of opposition is also mistaken. It should be defined in terms of the accountability of leadership to an electorate which has the power to remove that leadership. The mere existence of opposition without accountability does not ensure democracy. Insofar as the employer is only minimally accountable to the unions or to his workers for decisions which lie outside the immediate job area a trade union opposition does not constitute a sufficient condition for genuine industrial democracy. Finally, Blumberg argues that if trade unions have no power to replace the present government of industry but are simply able to challenge management in carefully delineated spheres of activity, most centrally the job area, then 'there is no pluralism, no choice, no alternative, no opposition, in short no democracy' (p. 146).

Goldthorpe has also criticised the analysis lying behind Donovan and the notion that the reforms proposed would increase industrial democracy. He suggests that in the post-war period management authority was not eroded, and argues that it is necessary to make a clear distinction between authority and power. 'If authority is understood, in the manner of Max Weber, as referring to the "legitimate exercise of command" it is in fact by no means evident that the authority of management has been reduced in any dramatic way' (Goldthorpe, 1977, p. 192). Managerial authority in the industrial enterprise 'stems on the one hand from the manager's status as the agent of the employer, and on the other from the contract of employment in which workers have engaged.' (p. 192) In the economic and social context of the post-war period management's control over labour had been weakened but this is to be understood not as a decline in authority but in management's *de facto* capacity to secure the compliance of workers with its specific requirements. 'Workers can now often prevent management from using its power in an entirely arbitrary or summary fashion; they can compel managements to negotiate and bargain with them on a widening range of issues; and in these ways and other ways they are able to call into question managerial "prerogatives", the exercise of which in the past must be seen not so much as an act of legitimate command but rather as the expression of a superior power position.' (p. 194). The Donovan analysis suggests particular developments of collective bargaining as a means of institutionalising the conflict arising from increased worker power, and thus 'no challenge is raised against management's ultimate responsibility for the conduct of an enterprise and for the definition of its goals.' (p. 190).

More fundamentally Goldthorpe has argued that the analysis lying behind Donovan was basically misconceived. Following Durkheim he argues that it is not possible to create a rational system of rewards and procedures in industry in the face of a wider structure of inequality which has no rationale whatsoever (Goldthorpe 1974). He suggests that whilst the Donovan proposals might have led to more formal rationality in the workplace they would not have produced a more stable normative system. Such a system could only be achieved through norms being supported by some minimum degree of value consensus, but such a consensus could not be achieved in the face of social, economic and organisational inequality. One element of that inequality is inequality in access to and control over decision-making processes. In that sense, if the aim is to create a new normative order in industry, then the extension of collective bargaining is not the way forward; the way forward is through changes in the authority structure of the enterprise.

In a limited way that process had already started by the end of the sixties, through the intervention of the state and the creation of a series of rights for workers and trade unions. Marshall has argued that Britain can be categorised according to two different but related systems for arranging relationships between the members of the community. One system is the market which distributes rewards unequally and creates class relationships; the other, the system of citizenship, Marshall saw as a system which would modify the market (Marshall, 1963, pp. 67-127). Citizenship meant that all members of the national society enjoyed a common body of civil, political and social rights; this system offset to some degree the inequalities of the class system. Marshall argued that the rights of citizenship had appeared in three stages in Britain: civil rights (e.g. freedom from arbitrary arrest) arose in the eighteenth century, political rights (the right to vote) in the nineteenth, while the twentieth century saw the emergence of social rights (e.g. the entitlement to free education and health care). In addition to these main elements of citizenship Marshall argued that a secondary system of 'industrial citizenship' had also been developing through the growth of trade unionism and the development of collective bargaining.

From the mid-1960s, as industrial crisis and industrial conflict developed in symbiotic relationship, government, managements and unions began to look with various degrees of reluctance at wider issues. The process began of transforming this secondary citizenship into a positive category of industrial rights. These were rights not simply to contest the distribution of rewards, but rights in the production process itself. This was apparent in the series of pieces of legislation establishing employees' rights in jobs, and the rights of trade unions to be recognised, and to be able to demand information from the firm, that we have noted earlier. It was also apparent in the demands of trade unions to be involved in decision-making processes at the governmental level of the firm, in the setting up of the Bullock Committee and the publication of the government's White Paper to consider ways of allowing trade unions to be involved in boardroom decision making. Goldthorpe has argued that this 'new thrust of citizenship in its ongoing war with class, is specifically aimed against the idea, coeval with capitalism, of labour as a commodity.' (Goldthorpe, 1978, p. 203).

The trade unions had from the middle 1960s onwards modified their position on participation. During the immediate post-war period they had articulated a view similar to Clegg's, that collective bargaining and permanent opposition were the sole means of achieving industrial democracy. By the mid-sixties, however, that position had begun to change. The TUC in its evidence to the Donovan Commission argued that the conflict of interest between employees and management did not present an overriding obstacle to worker representation at board level or indeed at other levels in the management hierarchy. The evidence made a distinction between the negotiating function of the employer and the general task of management. It argued that it did not detract from the independence of the trade unions for trade unionists to participate in the affairs of management until the stage when any of these affairs become a negotiable question (TUC, 1966). By the early 1970s the TUC had further developed its thinking on participation in management. It was arguing that whilst collective bargaining was adequate for most purposes, there was a range of decisions taken which affected employees which were outside and beyond the reaches of collective bargaining. It argued that there should be an extension of the collective bargaining function and a statutory obligation on companies to disclose a wide range of information to the unions; it also advocated the creation of a two-tier board system with half the members of the supervisory board coming from the workforce (TUC, 1974).

There were other influences at work. Britain's entry into the EEC in 1973 meant that both Government and industry had to take account of moves within the EEC related to worker participation, on which a variety of EEC proposals have a bearing. The draft statute for a European Company was originally submitted to the Council of Ministers in 1970. It proposed, *inter alia*, a two-tier board with one third employee participation on the upper supervisory tier, and also a works council in each European company. This draft statute is still under discussion a decade later. The draft Fifth Directive on company law was issued in 1972. It provides for the representation of employees on the boards of public companies employing more than 500 people; worker representatives would sit on the supervisory board, of which they would constitute one third. The management board is required to seek the approval of the supervisory board on major decisions (e.g. closure, reorganisation) and to report to it regularly on the progress of the business. The fifth directive is still under consideration by the legal affairs committee of the European Parliament.

More recently, in 1980, a new draft directive has been proposed on 'procedures for informing and consulting employees in undertakings with a complex structure, in particular trans-national undertakings' (the Vredeling/Davignon proposals). These require managements in complex undertakings to provide information, at least every six months, to employee representatives, which would provide a clear picture of the activities of the concern as a whole (including all of its subsidiaries worldwide) on such things as structure, manning, economic position, investment plans, and rationalisation plans. It also requires companies to engage in prior consultation, 'with a view to reaching agreement', about major decisions which are liable to affect employee interests directly, such as plant closure and changes in the activities or organisation of the plant.

Whilst none of the European proposals has, at the time of writing, attained the force of law, and discussion on them seems interminable, they have affected the political climate in the UK in interesting ways. Elliot provides a key illustration of this. After the UK joined the EEC in 1972 Government was worried that unless it moved quickly 'it would be swamped by alien policies'. The Department of Employment therefore wrote to both the TUC and CBI asking for their views on two-tier boards and worker directors. The TUC used the opportunity to go beyond the EEC proposals and demand 50% of the seats on the supervisory boards. Management bodies were forced to react and to begin to consider as a central possibility something that had previously been peripheral and arcane (Elliot, 1978, pp. 212-30).

The 1974 Labour government had pledged in its election manifesto that it would introduce an industrial democracy act. Instead it set up a committee of enquiry to look at ways of achieving boardroom participation. The report of this committee of enquiry under Lord Bullock was published in early

1977. The majority Bullock Report suggested a comprehensive extension of union rights, compelling companies employing more than 2,000 workers to have worker directors who would be appointed through trade union channels. Company boards would have to be reconstituted to consist of equal numbers of management and union representatives plus a minority of outside directors. (This is discussed further in Chapter Six). The subsequent White Paper in modifying these proposals suggested that employers in firms with over 500 employees should be obliged to discuss all major business decisions affecting employees before these decisions were taken, that the forum for these discussions should be a Joint Representative Committee, and that where such committees were not set up voluntarily by employers there should be a statutory fallback right for unions to demand them. The White Paper also suggested that in companies with over 2,000 employees, if employees wished to be represented on a supervisory board, they should have the right to claim representation; this right however could only come into operation four years after a Joint Representative Committee had been established and after a ballot of all employees had voted in favour of such a move; the percentage of employees who had to be in favour was left open in the White Paper. The Labour government had not introduced legislation when it was removed from office in 1979. The new Conservative administration were opposed to boardroom participation; they were however committed by their manifesto to encourage employee involvement in industry through consultation, communication and financial involvement. They were not committed to legislate on the topic.

The re-emergence of joint consultation

British management in the private sector, as represented by their various associations, was vehemently opposed to the Bullock proposals and the White Paper. There were however a small number of firms in the private sector who had worker director schemes and in the nationalised industries the Steel Corporation had introduced worker directors onto its regional boards in 1969 and its main board in 1976. By the mid-1970s the Post Office had also introduced employee representatives onto its decision making bodies at national, regional and area levels. (See Chapter Six). Interest in participation had nevertheless increased amongst management generally from the late sixties. In 1968 the British Institute of Management announced that 'in a highly industrialised society forced to undergo technological change and to find new ways of holding if not raising the standard of living people feel that democratic processes work badly. It creates unrest and tension; radical relief will be required to avoid an explosion. We need not look far abroad to see the dangers. Soon we must take new measures to realise the main ideals of industrial democracy whilst safeguarding the wealth producing industrial framework.' (BIM, 1968). By 1973 the CBI had produced a report which, whilst firmly underlining the need to retain managerial perogative, argued that there was a need to develop a wider degree of participation in the process of decision-making throughout British industry. This was to be done by establishing joint consultation at plant level and company councils at company level (CBI, 1973).

As we saw in the last chapter the enthusiasm for formal consultative structures in the immediate post-war period appeared thereafter to decline. Thus McCarthy, writing in the mid 1960s, argued that the rise of collective bargaining and the increase in the number and activities of shop stewards meant that unless joint consultative committees became essentially negotiating committees they would fall into disuse and decay; this he concluded had been the fate of the consultative movement (McCarthy, 1966, p. 33).

More recent evidence, on the other hand, points to a growth in consultative committees. National surveys carried out in 1972 and 1973 asked management respondents whether they had any joint committees or councils in which management and employee representatives met to discuss and settle problems. About 70% of respondents said that there were joint committees in their workplaces. Whilst this finding does not distinguish between consultation and negotiation Hawes and Brookes suggest that 'it is not inconsistent with a picture of growth' (Hawes and Brookes, 1980, p. 356). They also draw attention to the fact that administrative information collected by the Department of Employment in 300 firms in 1972 indicates that two-thirds had some form of consultative committee (p. 356). Knight recorded that in a 1976 survey of 300 firms with over 200 employees in manufacturing industry personnel managers reported that just over half of the establishments had a workplace-wide consultative committee covering all employees and another 23% had one covering all manual workers. About 50% of the firms had company-wide consultative arrangements and in just over half of these the committee was wholly or partly union-based. Likewise at establishment level just over half the committees were based on trade union representation in whole or in part (Knight, 1979, pp. 35-9).

Another survey carried out in 1977, in which personnel managers were interviewed in workplaces in manufacturing industries, found that in 42% of the establishments covered joint management and employee consultative committees of some description existed (Beaumont and Deaton, 1981). Over half these committees had been established within the five years previous to the survey. The researchers' conclusion was that 'overall our result suggests that not only are joint consultative committees on the increase in Britain, but they are becoming increasingly heterogeneous in nature both in terms of the characteristics of the plants where they are established and in terms of their performance as viewed by management.' (p. 68). A related survey carried out two years later, in 1979, but this time in the service sector, suggested that with the exception of the construction industry just over 40% of establishments had joint consultative committees. In construction only 16% of establishments had joint consultative committees. Respondents were asked whether these committees had been set up within the last five years. Leaving aside the construction industry, 57% of respondents said that they had, a surprisingly similar figure to that from manufacturing industry (Hawes and Smith, 1981).

The most comprehensive evidence on the extent of joint consultation comes from a survey of workplace industrial relations carried out in 1980 (Daniel and Millward, 1983). This survey, unlike previous ones, covered all sectors of industry apart from mining and agriculture. It found that across all industry there were consultative arrangements reported by management in 37% of establishments. The project however covered those at establishments with more than 25 employees. The authors note that the proportion of establishments with consultative committees increases with size of establishment. Using a cut-off point similar to those used in other surveys would therefore increase the proportion of establishments with consultative committees. The survey also shows that 'where consultative machinery existed it was four times more likely to exist alongside collective bargaining machinery than it was to exist on its own.' (ibid). The authors suggest that in unionised workplaces consultative committees may tend to become an adjunct of collective bargaining if the union is well established and an alternative channel of communications if the union is weak.

Whilst the different sampling frames and low response rates in some of the earlier surveys make it difficult to estimate change over time with accuracy the general trend from the figures presented seems to indicate an increase over the period of the 1970s in the number of consultative committees. This is confirmed by other data from the 1980 survey, in which information about the introduction and demise of consultative committees was collected and analysed. 'The results indicated a clear pattern of growth with establishments with recently introduced committees outnumbering those in which committees had been abandoned by nine to one.' (ibid). The growth rate of committees appears to have been greater outside manufacturing industry, particularly in the private service sector.

Further and more detailed evidence and some explanation of the pattern is provided by Cressey and his colleagues, who carried out research on participation in 1979 in 'all private sector enterprises which based their UK operations in Scotland and had more than 500 employees' (Cressey et al., 1981, p. 3). Research was carried out in 48 enterprises, sampled to represent the above universe, and interviews took place with both managers and worker representatives. Fifty per cent of the enterprises had one or more consultative committees, with stronger representation of consultative committees in manufacturing than in the service sector. Only 17% of the consultative committees were not trade union based. 'Results suggested that consultation was usually an established part of union-management relations and not simply an alternative to unionisation or a sign of its weakness.' (p. 17).

Cressey and his colleagues suggest that their data support the notion that there had been a resurgence of consultation. In looking at the reasons for this they found that the following factors were important. Most of the schemes that they studied had been set up or revised at the initiative of management. Participation was a 'live topic' for management, partly because of the threats of legislation from the EEC and from Westminster and partly because, and in relation to that, the CBI and a number of employer bodies were advocating voluntary developments of consultation. Thus it seems that part of the reason for the renaissance of consultation is that 'it represents action by managers to pursue their concept of industrial democracy and participation, both for its own sake and as a response to the threat of legislation' (p.54).

The second factor they saw as explaining the resurgence of consultation was the onset of economic uncertainty and recession. In times of economic stress for individual firms, the authors argue, the unions make more strident demands for information in the face of employment uncertainty, and adverse market conditions create a need for management to emphasise that differences should be put aside, management and workforce uniting in the face of common adversity. A further factor which Cressey and his colleagues suggest is responsible for the resurgence of consultation is the influence of government pay policy and, in particular, the encouragement through pay policy of self-financing productivity deals. This leads to the setting up of special committees to discuss and monitor progress. Quite often, the authors suggest, 'these are widened into a range of job-related issues concerned with job performance and work organisation and sometimes, depending on the nature of the arrangement, with the performance of the company.' (p.54).

Whilst Cressey and his colleagues are clear that there has been a resurgence in consultation, they argue that not all consultation is of the same character. They identify two main types of arrangement. In the first, consultation acts as a substitute for or an avenue to collective bargaining, and has a decision-making or quasi-decision-making function. In the second, there is no decision-making and the committees are characterised as simply being involved in communications exercises. However, these exercises, although manifestly without much purpose, do (they suggest) have latent functions. For management they provide an activity which gives the appearance of 'doing something about participation' and an opportunity to show that they are concerned with trying to solve enterprise problems. This helps to develop 'enterprise, as opposed to class, consciousness' amongst the workforce. In this way it legitimates management's current role and their authority. But quite often this form of committee also has some attractions for the trade unions who have no particular wish to move the frontiers of control forward from the joint regulation of job decisions; for them consultation provides some minor support for the current state of collective bargaining without imposing the strain of expanding the scope of this bargaining. The implication the authors draw is that in so far as consultation is an accommodation of interests, the accommodation is more successful for managers than for the workforce, 'as it provides an opportunity to educate the representatives in the problems of management and helps secure their cooperation with management objectives' (p. 56). The corresponding lack of success of representatives 'can be attributed to a vicious circle of institutional and structural impediments to their organisational ability to tackle issues beyond the normal range of job decisions and still be accountable, and the lack of training, expertise and interest in the question compared with management's, partly because of a realistic appreciation of the limits of what could be achieved in the face of opposition by managers to any threat to their right to manage.' (p. 56). They suggest that while the renaissance in joint consultation may appear to increase participation 'its development may act to forestall rather than foster any real change either in representatives' or employees' influence in the decision-making process.' (p. 57).

Conclusion

As one moves from a broad historical approach to looking in more detail at one period the complexities of worker participation become more apparent. After the second world war Britain, along with other western market economies, entered a period of economic growth, stability and high employment; this was associated with rapid technological development and industrial and occupational change, the growth and development of the welfare state, and rising standards of living. These conditions favoured the market power of labour which was manifested in the growth of the shop steward movement and localised collective bargaining, and which was focused, with apparent success, on distributionalist issues. The 'affluent' society was thought to have arrived. As the cracks began to appear within the economic system during the 1960s, however, increasing public concern was expressed about the industrial relations system and the beginnings of changes of emphasis within it.

Whilst Donovan sought to formalise the exercise of trade union power through collective bargaining, within the trade unions there was a movement towards challenging managerial rights in the sphere of production and constraining the exercise of management authority. The public manifestations of this appeared in a change of stance towards being involved in the authority structures of the enterprise and in demands for individual and collective rights for workers in the sphere of employment. Government made some concession to these demands through legislation and the setting-up of the Bullock Committee to consider the issue of boardroom participation. Management also responded through an increased willingness to engage in public discussion of participation and by setting up a variety of consultative and participative mechanisms at the workplace. By the 1970s therefore a new wave of interest in participation was under way. In the following chapters we look in more detail at the stances of both labour and management towards participation, some of the factors that underpin these, and its implications in practice for the authority structure of the enterprise and its operation.

Further Reading

Clegg (1980) again furnishes an important source of institutional description. Clarke et al. (1972) review post-war developments in participation till the late 1960s; Elliott (1978) provides a detailed account of the contemporary history leading up to the Bullock Report and of its immediate aftermath. An interesting account of the same period, which contrasts developments in the British and the German trade union movements, is contained in Clark et al. (1980). Broader and more theoretical accounts of developments in post-war industrial relations are to be found in Fox and Flanders (1969), Goldthorpe (1977 and 1978) and Brown (1978).

4 · Worker Orientations and Work Situations

Much industrial relations writing on participation and industrial democracy concentrates on procedures, rules and institutions, and ignores the sociology of the workplace and indeed the sociology of the labour market. Moreover it is particularly through concentrating on institutions that writers such as Clegg were able to look back over the previous century and argue that the institutions which had developed to look after the interests of the labour movement were industrial democracy achieved (Clegg, 1960). The development of the institutions of industrial relations have been continuous and almost linear (with regressive periods in the early years of the century and again in the early 1980s). By contrast, as we have seen in earlier chapters, the frontier of control between management and workers has shifted, assaults on it have been discontinuous, and the pattern of advances and retreats complex.

In addition, as Ford has argued, 'writers on worker participation, industrial democracy and self management have at least one thing in common with writers on management; that is, with a few notable exceptions they tend to assume a monocultural workforce.' (Ford 1978). They also tend to assume that the workforce is homogeneous in other respects, whereas in any organisation it is in fact differentiated by occupation, by skill level, by the technology and production process, by the payments system, by its geographical distribution within the workplace, and (where it exists) by trade union membership. These factors arise out of the social organisation of work within the enterprise. It is also differentiated by factors which are socially constructed outside the workplace; that is, by bio-social factors such as age, sex, and race; and also by religion and by common or diverse community situations.

From the perspective of worker participation, divisions which exist within the workforce, whether deriving from inside or outside the work situation, are likely to produce a variety of orientations towards participation, different participatory strategies and differential access to support for these strategies. Walker has suggested that the determinants of workers' participation can be divided into situation factors – that is, structural features of the workplace such as technology, which create the *potential* for participation – and human factors, that is, attitudes and capabilities, which produce different *propensities* for participation (Walker, 1974, p. 13).

However, propensity to participate might be seen both to arise from and to influence structural features of the workplace; in addition features of the wider economy and non-work related matters may also affect propensity. 'The willingness and ability of the actors to participate cannot easily be separated from the structure or "potential" of the situation in which these feelings are shaped.' (Loveridge, 1980, p. 299). In the first part of this chapter we consider the literature on some of these issues; in the second, we look at recent research on the attitudes of workers and their representatives towards participation.

Worker orientations

The relationship of the worker to the production process has been a central concern of both industrial sociology and industrial psychology. The progress of theorising in these disciplines, as we noted in Chapter Two, has not been unconnected to historical developments. The work of F. W. Taylor and the scientific management school which grew round his work rested on the assumption that the average worker has an inherent dislike of work and will avoid it if he or she can (Taylor, 1947). Because of this the worker must be coerced into working through a system of sanctions based on economic incentives. The average worker prefers to be directed rather than to think for her- or himself; providing that the systems of direction and control and of economic incentives are correct then the worker will be suitably productive. There is no room in this model for worker participation, though as we have seen in Chapter One the managerial techniques it gave rise to did have the unanticipated effect of allowing the informal exercise of worker controls on the production process.

An important source for an alternative model to that of Taylor came from the research which Roethlisberger and Dickson and their colleagues undertook in the Hawthorne plant of the General Electric company between the late 1920s and the mid 1930s. This emphasised that industrial workers should not be seen as isolated individuals who act in a calculative way in relation to work simply to maximise income, but rather as social animals who are influenced in their behaviour by interaction with other workers —particularly their immediate work group — and by the formal interaction they enter into with management, especially their immediate supervisor. Styles of leadership and group participation in decision-making over work tasks were seen as important within this model in motivating workers towards higher productivity (see also Chapter Seven). Subsequently, within this body of socio-psychological theorising a more complex analysis has been developed. Often labelled 'the neo-human relations approach', it postulates that man is a wanting animal with an ascending order of needs: from basic physiological needs and the need for safety and security to social and affiliative needs followed by those for ego satisfaction and status; finally at the top of the pyramid there are self actualisation needs, that is drives to use one's full potential and creative capacity. Under the conditions of modern industrial life, according to this analysis, the creative potentials of the average worker are only partially used. In order to obtain commitment managers need to create working conditions in which the worker's higher order needs are satisfied (Maslow, 1943, McGregor, 1960). A variant on this theme was elaborated by Herzberg who argued that the individual worker will have a positive attitude to work if factors creating dissatisfaction (e.g. bad working conditions) are removed from the work situation and motivating factors such as those towards recognition and achievement are developed (Herzberg, 1966).

The development of much work in the field of direct participation (job enrichment, job enlargement, autonomous work groups, quality circles) stems from, or is related to, these approaches. Whilst they present a theory of the individual worker which leads to an attempt to humanise work, the basic aim is to reconcile individual motivation with organisational purposes at the level of the work task. The wider organisational setting is not seen as a legitimate object for worker participation. Herzberg, for example, has argued that 'to expect individuals at lower levels of an organisation to exercise control over the establishment of overall goals is unrealistic' (Herzberg et al., 1959).

An important theoretical criticism which has been made of the neo-human relations approach is that one cannot proceed from a general specification of individual human needs to the wants and expectations of particular individuals (Goldthorpe et al., 1969). Chapter One outlined how the technological or production system, a system largely ignored by human relations and neo-human relations researchers, has been seen as acting as an important constraint on or determinant of attitudes and behaviour in the workplace. Blauner, it will be remembered, argued that technology was of crucial importance for the attitudes and behaviour of workers (Blauner, 1964). He saw it as having a central bearing on the amount of control and degree of meaning that work had for the individual worker, and for the possibilities of social interaction and self fulfilment which work offered. Whilst these had reached their nadir in assembly line technology, process production, in his view, would lead to an increase in workers' control over the immediate work process and produce meaningful work in a more cohesive and integrated industrial climate. The technological determinist approach led Mallet to rather different conclusions about the effect of process production (Mallet, 1975). Through creating new types of skill and of knowledge amongst workers in the advanced industries it would, he argued, create a new kind of working class which would have positive orientations to control not only at the level of the enterprise but also at the level of the economy. The mechanism of this process is not indicated and indeed, as Gallie has written of both Blauner and Mallet, 'It is difficult to avoid the feeling that the data basis on which these theories rest is perilously frail.' (Gallie, 1978, p. 29).

The same writer has argued, on the basis of a comparative study of chemical plants in France and Britain, that 'the work of most of the operators was substantially less advantageous than Blauner suggested and the most common attitude towards work in our refineries was one of indifference. It is extremely doubtful whether automation leads to the overcoming of alienation in work in any profound sense of the term.' (Gallie, 1978, p. 296). Gallie's study argues persuasively that technology is not the dominant determinant of attitudes and behaviour. 'Instead our evidence indicates the critical importance of the wider cultural and social structural patterns of specific societies for determining the nature of social interaction within the advance sector.' (p. 295).

The limitations of a technological determinist approach were also pointed out by Goldthorpe and his colleagues. In a study of three plants with different technologies in the same area of Britain they found similarities of orientation and work behaviour. Moreover the process workers in the sample 'were if anything less concerned than men in other groups with possibilities for "participation" in plant or in work affairs more generally'. In the assembly plant that they studied, whilst the objective features of the work situation should have given rise to work dissatisfaction, the car workers they interviewed did not define their work situation in this way. They recognised for example that their jobs were boring but nevertheless expressed overall satisfaction. This was explained in terms of car workers having a prior orientation to work, defined as instrumental, which led them to see work simply as a means to financial rather than any other type of rewards. Goldthorpe and his colleagues argued that 'The effects of technologically determined conditions of work are always *mediated* through the meanings that men give to their work and through their own definitions of their work situation, and because these meanings and definitions in turn *vary* with the particular sets of wants and expectations that men bring to their employment.' (Goldthorpe et al., 1969, p. 182). The propensity to accept work as a means to extrinsic ends was thus understood as something 'that to an important degree existed independently of and prior to their involvement in the present work situation' (ibid.).

Goldthorpe and his colleagues tended to stress the community and family situation of workers as the central source of work orientations; this was in direct contrast to those following a technological implications approach who looked at workers' behaviour purely in terms of variables operating within the factory gates. Other research shows that differing orientations and attitudes to work will prevail in differing contexts. Daniel, for example, has argued that 'It is not legitimate to project priorities derived from one situation, for instance the decision to take a particular job, onto a quite different situation, for instance the response to events, the changes and stimuli in the workplace itself.' (Daniel, 1973.) Beynon and Blackburn have shown that although workers may have certain orientations when they are seeking employment, once they are in a work situation they make important accommodations and adjustments as their experience is influenced by work processes, pay levels and the power structure within the enterprise (Beynon and Blackburn, 1972). They also point out that orientations are influenced by biographical factors in the worker's life outside the factory. A number of studies, for example, have shown that young workers' orientations change between the period immediately after leaving school and their early 20s when they are entering the period of courtship and marriage (Carter, 1975). Other studies have shown that the work orientations of women workers change at different points in the life and fertility cycles (Martin and Roberts, 1983).

In reviewing the post-war British empirical studies of worker orientations Brown and his colleagues have concluded that because for most of the economically active in our society work is a necessity, orientations towards it are bound to be, at least in part, instrumental and concerned with economic rewards (Brown et al., 1983). Nevertheless, an instrumental orientation to work need not, and typically does not, exclude a keen interest in other features of the job and work situation. Whilst the economic rewards from work were the dominant feature for most groups of workers studied, nevertheless, 'in almost all the studies we have considered, in addition to economic rewards and prospects attention has been given to the intrinsic nature of the job itself, the conditions under which it is carried out, and the social relations at work, as potential or actual sources of satisfaction or dissatisfaction.' (ibid.). The studies show, the authors suggest, that there are differences in work orientations between different categories of workers, the most important being gender and stage in the age and family life cycles. Industry and occupational level also appear to play a part.

Economic orientations are strongest for prime age males in manual occupations. The young and those in professional and skilled non-manual occupations tended to stress intrinsic orientations the most. Women workers in the 26-45 age range and men over 45 tended to stress convenience factors as did many in unskilled and semi-skilled work. Brown and his colleagues conclude that 'the differences we observed between the orientations of men and women, full and part time workers, employed and unemployed, different social classes and age groups indicate the complexity of assessing global orientations to work and the dangers of generalising from particular populations to the whole.' (ibid.). They nevertheless found some evidence that, in the current recession, orientations towards work have become more narrowly preoccupied with pay and security and similar 'economistic' considerations. This bears out the general proposition in Chapter Two that general labour market considerations affect the way the workforce reacts to employment. It also leads us to consider the way in which specific labour market situations affect the way in which workers view work.

Market situation

The labour market situation of workers is likely to affect both their general orientations towards work and the degree of actual and potential control that they have over their own situation. One way of approaching this issue is through the concept of labour market segmentation, which sees the labour market as being divided up into a number of discrete and largely non-competing groups. Ryan makes a distinction between pre-market segmentation and in-market segmentation (Ryan, 1981). The former refers to the factors that affect the attributes that particular social strata bring with them when they enter the labour market, the latter to the differentiation of opportunities within the labour market.

The social processes which operate to channel people into the labour market are complex and inter-related. The initial entry into work is of vital importance for an individual's subsequent ability to sell his or her labour power so as to secure a particular level of goods, living conditions and personal life experience. Initial job entry is a 'ticket for a life journey'. The allocation of this ticket initially is determined by social, structural and cultural factors in the home, school and community (Brannen, 1975). The educational process operates so as to channel individuals into particular sectors of the labour market. It provides knowledge, skills and attitudes conducive to success or failure. For some it heightens aspirations and expectations, while for others it cools out aspiration and provides a self-image which fits with the characteristics of lower echelon jobs (ibid.).

In-market segmentation represents the continuation of these processes into the labour market itself. The most elementary form in which in-market segmentation is conceptualised is one in which a distinction is made between primary and secondary labour markets. 'The primary sector contains good jobs, which offer relatively high wages, good working conditions, substantial job security, chances of career advancement, and due process in the administration of work rules. The secondary sector has poor jobs, which offer inferior social status, low wages, and poor working conditions. These jobs are also dead end, insecure and involve a highly personalistic, often capricious relationship between supervisor and subordinate. Particular groups, such as women, ethnic and racial minorities, and immigrants are confined to secondary jobs and this explains their disadvantaged economic position.' (Piore, 1980, p. 380). Bosanquet and Doeringer have argued that in the case of Britain available evidence pointed to two main groupings, women and blacks, as being over-represented in the secondary labour market (Bosanquet and Doeringer, 1973). More recently work by Hakim has shown that the occupational segregation of women into secondary labour market type jobs has persisted in a relatively unchanged way over the last century and that recent equal opportunity legislation has done little to change the pattern (Hakim, 1979). Other work has shown that black workers are more likely to suffer unemployment than white workers both as a result of the types of jobs they have and of patterns of discrimination in the labour market (Smith, 1981).

More recent developments in the exploration of labour market segmentation have argued that the simple dualism described above does not provide an adequate account. Reich and his colleagues have further divided the primary sector into subordinate and independent jobs: the former are those in which the skills are specific to the firm, and therefore dependent on the existence of an internal market, the latter are those that are occupation specific (Reich et al., 1973). Kreckel conceives of the labour market as composed of a number of distinct sub-markets which are hierarchically ordered, and separated by more or less rigid barriers to mobility of both a vertical and horizontal kind. 'The sum total of these labour market "allotments" is fitted in mosaic-like fashion into a symmetrically shaped opportunity structure which narrows down to a bottle neck towards the top. It is in these upper regions of the occupational opportunity structure that success becomes increasingly more restricted.' (Kreckel, 1980, p. 534).

Following from this it is possible to conceive of a variety of labour market segments. Within the primary sector, occupational groups which have academic, professional or managerial skills, and which control entry through professional associations and a variety of forms of 'credentialism', sit at the top of the hierarchy. Below them are groupings of technical and skilled workers which have restricted entry based on technical qualifications or apprenticeship. These groupings form the independent sectors of the primary market; they have generally marketable qualifications, though the degree of marketability will vary both across groups and through time. Within the subordinate sectors of the primary market, that is those that are specific to particular organisations or groups of organisations, there will also be a variety of skill levels and degrees of closure.

The secondary sector may also be seen as being composed of a variety of segments. At the top there are groups of semi- and unskilled workers who exist as a 'pool' of labour within large organisations and who sit on the borderline between internal and external markets. At the bottom of the hierarchy are a group (small in Britain) of illegal immigrants who have no residence or citizenship rights and who exist invisibly in the labour market. In the middle there are the groups with whom the secondary labour market literature has largely dealt, who tend to be segregated by sex, age or ethnic origin. These groups are often seen, and to some extent see themselves, as marginal to the labour market, in the sense of having available to them an alternative, albeit 'second best' role outside the labour market. 'They are expected to be able to retire to their pensions or into institutions, to their countries of origin or into their households.' (Kreckel, p. 538).

There is a diversity of models of labour market segmentation and this is not the place to attempt either a critique or a synthesis. The segmentation pattern set out above is incomplete in that it does not differentiate, for example, between national and local labour markets or between public and private sectors. For our purposes however it does at least highlight the fact that different groups in the labour market are differentially placed in their ability to control their own occupational position and, following from this, to relate to employers and to their employment situation. At the bottom of the hierarchy of markets are workers who are isolated from each other, who have few rights, work in insecure employment, and who come nearest to the Marxian notion of a reserve army of labour. They have few resources for and little orientation towards any form of control over their work situation. As one moves up the segments there is an increase in organisation and control exerted through occupational associations (including trade unions), the formalised structures of internal markets or internal customary arrangements.

The main dynamic behind the development of labour market segmentation is to be found in two inter-linked processes within western industrial society; the increasing need to plan and control labour as a factor of production, and the increasing power of parts of the labour force to disrupt and frustrate planning. Precisely the same dynamic, we have suggested in earlier chapters, lies behind the development of worker participation, which can be interpreted here as the last resort of a frustrated management or the thrusting forward of a self-confident trade union movement. In either case the groups most affected are likely to be in the primary sector: as far as the employers are concerned because this is the sector of labour they wish to secure; and as far as the unions are concerned because this is where they are strongest. Secondary sector workers are cut out from this process. Moreover labour legislation, by providing well organised workers with increased opportunities for protection, and by often excepting from its coverage unstable areas of employment or small employers, increases this segmentation. In that sense worker participation has been in the past and is likely to remain something for the fat cats on both the workers' and employers' sides of industry, and may well therefore increase labour market inequalities.

Workers' attitudes towards participation

This is not to argue that within the primary sector there is an unambiguous or undirectional orientation towards participation. What we have said earlier about worker orientations suggests that this would be unlikely. The primary sector nevertheless provides the situation of fullest potential. We now go on to look at some recent British studies of the orientations and attitudes of workers and shop stewards towards participation. This data was collected during a period (1970-79) when there was extensive public discussion and political debate about a variety of forms of worker participation but particularly about worker directors (see Chapter Six). It is however subject to a number of constraints. Firstly, there is no data on the orientations of blacks or women towards participation. The enquiries of industrial sociologists and industrial relations researchers have not strayed much beyond the primary sector. Secondly, most research has not tried to relate what industrial sociology has taught us about variations in orientation to work and the factors that affect that, to attitudes and behaviour in the institutions of participation. This means that there can be no clear connections between the data presented in this part of the section and what has been said earlier. Nevertheless, some broadly parallel analytical points emerge later.

One of the few programmes of research which have tried to look at worker orientation, the sources of work orientation and attitudes to participation, was carried out by a group at Aston University between 1976 and 1979. They studied workplace industrial relations in four Midlands manufacturing companies, all of which were unionised with collective bargaining arrangements and which were at different stages in a movement towards the establishment of a works council system of employee participation. Marchington suggests in a monograph describing one of the companies, which he calls 'Kitchenco', that 'Priorities are very much geared towards extrinsic rather than intrinsic factors, and for this reason, we would estimate that participation would only attract a moderate level of interest.' (Marchington, 1980, p. 46).

Loveridge and his colleagues show that whilst there were differences between plants and within plants, the predominant work orientation gave high value to financial rewards; this was given as the main reason for joining the firm, the main reason for remaining in the job, and the main reason for considering leaving, by the majority of workers. Job security and good physical working conditions were also highly valued (Loveridge et al.). However, intrinsic work satisfactions such as having control over tasks, and variation in work, were also valued by some categories, particularly by older manual skilled operatives; this category 'displayed distinctly solidaristic orientations to work with strong group loyalties and attachments to the firm' (ibid.). Craftsmen were also solidaristic but with attachment to an external occupational union rather than to the firm.

Regarding attitudes to participation, Loveridge found that across all companies the majority of respondents wanted more say in their work; but the focus of this desire for increased participation was at the task level only. Likewise across all companies the majority of respondents wanted more information, but there was a higher degree of demand for information at the section or departmental level, i.e. the job level, than at more distant levels of the organisational hierarchy. Within this overall pattern there were variations. Skilled workers and those placing value on the intrinsic rewards of their jobs were more likely than other respondents to be interested in information on company or holding group performance. 'The highest strategic awareness was amongst male married employees in the higher skilled categories with longest company service and time in their present job.' (ibid.).

Marchington also looked at the degree and range of activities for which participation was desired. The majority of his employee respondents felt that decision-making should remain firmly within the realms of management, though there was a desire for a greater degree of participation than currently existed. Looking at the decision-making process in areas which ranged from the immediate task to policies on new products, he concludes; 'items which attract the most interest are those that have traditionally been within the ambit of employees and this interest reduces as the subject becomes more abstract... For most employees, control over decision-making is not of paramount importance unless it is closely concerned with one's own job; and even then there is no great desire for total control.' (Marchington, 1980, p. 48). Across all four companies there was felt to be little demand for forms of participation such as worker directors or full worker ownership; there was however support for extensions of collective bargaining, increases in information and profit-sharing. What support there was for worker directors or for ideas of worker control was confined to young, male, less skilled workers (Loveridge et al.).

This general picture is born out by the work of Heller and his colleagues who undertook a national household survey of 1725 people in full employment and combined this with a field study in 14 plants (Heller et al., 1979). They looked at the degree of actual involvement in decision-making in relation to desired involvement over 16 decision areas ranging from task organisation to departmental organisation, to broad policy decisions on investment. They concluded that 'The total amount of decision taking at work is astonishingly low,' and that 'There is little evidence that workers want to have a radically different degree of influence or control over decisions.' (p. 20). There was more demand for control over decisions close to their daily jobs than over decisions at departmental or company level.

These results contrast somewhat with those of a study undertaken in the steel industry at the beginning of the 1970s, in which a sample of 2379 manual, clerical, technical and supervisory workers in nine different plants were interviewed (Brannen et al., 1976). The steel industry was in the public sector (though recently nationalised), was highly unionised, and had an established system of collective bargaining, a developing system of joint consultation, and a system of worker directors. Respondents were all male, and the sample excluded trainee apprentices and others under 18. The manual sample included production workers, craftsmen, craftsmen's helpers and other semi- and unskilled indirect workers (e.g. drivers, crane-men). A very high proportion of the sample defined themselves as having a high degree of control over their immediate tasks; 60% said they could try out their own ideas on the job, 76% felt that they could control the pace at which they worked, 61% could move around on the job, 78% could take a breather when they wished. Nearly 60% of the sample thought their work was interesting all or most of the time and only 10% found no interest in their work. In Blauner's terms they showed a very low degree of alienation. Within the sample there was variation within items with supervisors, craftsmen, technicians and clerical workers showing the highest degree of autonomy and production workers the lowest (Brannen and Eldridge, 1973).

Looking now at their attitudes towards participation, 86% of the sample thought it important for workers to have some say in the way in which their plant was run, a similar proportion thought it important to have some say in the running of their department. However, 70% of respondents felt that in general management should be responsible for decision-making although they should consult workers before deciding. Looked at in relation to individual decision areas, the pattern was rather different. In a range of six decision areas, from day-to-day work organisation to financial policy and major changes in production methods, a majority of the sample thought that all areas, apart from wages and conditions, were currently areas of unilateral management prerogative. Wages and conditions were seen by the majority as jointly decided. When asked how decisions ought to be taken in these areas there was a general demand for more participation. In each of the six areas more than one-third of respondents felt that the decisions should be made jointly, except for wages where three-quarters felt that the matter should be jointly decided. This proportion varied, however, between issues and occupational groups. At the strategic level of decision-taking (financial policy, major changes in production methods), twice as many manual as white collar workers wanted joint decision-making, with unskilled and semi-skilled workers expressing stronger preferences than skilled workers. On issues of daily work organisation and use of contract workers the technical workers took up similar positions to manual workers. Supervisory and clerical workers were more strongly orientated towards managerial prerogative (Brannen and Eldridge, 1973).

Overall, then, there was a demand for more increased participation, with substantive minorities wanting joint decision-making at the strategic levels of the organisation. Three quarters of the sample of employees were in favour of the idea of worker directors. However, 'concern with the need for influence in the corridors of power and in macro-decisions on the part of workers we interviewed may well be exceptional, reflecting the particularly traumatic period which the steel industry was experiencing. Because of this the support for the idea of worker directors which we find may be greater than would otherwise be the case' (Brannen et al., 1976, p. 56). But when asked whether they thought that collective bargaining, joint consultation or worker directors gave the workforce the greatest influence over managerial decision-making, there was a very clear view that collective bargaining was the most effective way of exerting worker influence, followed by joint consultation; worker directors came a poor third (Brannen et al., 1973).

Shop stewards

We now turn to the views of shop stewards about participation. This will allow us broadly to compare the degree of similarity between workers and their representatives in their views of participation. Shop stewards in the steel industry had a much stronger view than their members that decision-making was largely a managerial prerogative in four of the six areas looked at; the exception was decisions about wages and conditions, which they were very clear was an area for joint decision-making and disciplinary action: less than one third thought it was a matter for unilateral management action (Brannen et al., 1973). There was also a clear demand for more participation. A majority thought that wages, conditions, discipline and use of contract labour should be matters for joint decision-making. With the exception of the area of financial policy the shop stewards took a more demanding stance than their constituents (ibid.).

Marchington also found that shop stewards in this sample were in general 'keener on increased participation in management decision-making than are ordinary employees. Whereas just 17% of the employee sample feel it important to prevent decisions being taken unless there is shop floor agreement nearly half the stewards (43%) desire this degree of participation' (Marchington 1980, p. 71). Regarding participation in relation to particular decisions he likewise found that in nearly every case the stewards were more interested in a greater say than their constituents. There was a very high correlation between the scores of the representatives and those of their constituents in the sense 'that when an employee desired greater participation in a particular issue so do their stewards.' (ibid., p. 73). He also found that 'issues which have traditionally fallen within the sphere of influence of employees and stewards, such as job related matters, bonus levels and aspects which affect it, attract a greater degree of interest. Again in line with the employee sample stewards are not particularly bothered about participation in more distant decisions such as those relating to pricing and new product policies' (p. 73).

Marchington concludes that stewards desire greater participation than their constituents in nearly all cases. However the types of issues in which they want some participation are very similar to those chosen by their constituents – notably job related aspects of employment. The views of stewards and constituents tend to be more similar if the issue is one which the shop floor values as important, but more diverse if it is one over which it desires little control. There is very little difference in the forms of participation desired by stewards and their workers, with worker directors and worker ownership being consistently rejected as feasible ideas. He concludes that most stewards and also most employees feel that actual participation at Kitchenco 'is considerably less than it ought to be although a small number of stewards believe it should not be increased' (p. 78).

Ursell and her colleagues also examined shop stewards' attitudes towards worker participation and the framework within which they considered it (Ursell et al., 1976). They interviewed 184 shop stewards drawn from a variety of industries and from both the public and the private sectors; the majority of their respondents were strongly in favour of 'industrial democracy' (the term Ursell used) and saw it as an issue of central importance. The majority also wanted more 'industrial democracy' than was currently practised. They saw collective bargaining as a major means of extending 'industrial democracy' with worker directors and work reorganisation only being favoured by a minority. The majority saw 'industrial democracy' working at both the level of the job and the level of the company. Manual shop stewards were more in favour of 'industrial democracy' than non-manual shop stewards. Those with a strong left wing political allegiance were more in favour of bargaining-related approaches to 'industrial democracy' than others. Younger shop stewards were more enthusiastic about 'industrial democracy' than older shop stewards and older stewards were more conservative in their views, being more satisfied with the existing order. The older shop stewards showed the strongest preference for the 'softer' approaches of work group meetings and job redesign. Fewer wanted worker directors on the board, they felt less need for organisations to share power more dramatically, and wanted less shop floor influence over decision-making at all organisational levels. 'This could indicate that people grow less demanding as they grow older. It is also possible that it reflects a general cultural change, with the aspirations and expectations of the younger generation of shop stewards being much higher. Either interpretation could be supported by the fact that age was strongly associated with political orientation, the younger individuals registering more strongly left wing views. Nevertheless age is still an important correlate since the relationships described above remain even where political orientation is held constant.' (p. 13).

More general data on shop stewards' attitudes to industrial democracy was collected through a national survey, carried out by the Government Social Survey, in 296 manufacturing companies with over 2000 employees. Up to three directors were interviewed in each company and in one establishment in each company up to four managers, a supervisor and three shop stewards (Knight, 1979). When asked to compare current levels of participation with desired levels over nine areas of decision-making, shop stewards saw broad policy decisions (capital investment, major changes in production methods) as very firmly an area of managerial prerogative; pay and safety as being an area of joint decision-making, conditions of work and welfare as tending in that direction; and other areas such as hours of work and discipline as being matters for joint discussion or joint decision. Over all areas, however, there was a desire for a greater increase in participation, with general policy matters such as capital investment and major changes in production being seen as areas of joint discussion/joint decision, and all others seen as very much subject to joint decision-making (ibid., Appendix D, Tables 40D to 48D).

Conclusion

This chapter has suggested that the attitudes of workers towards participation are likely to be related to their broader orientations towards work. Orientations to work are varied and will themselves be a function of the interaction of several factors, including family and community, market, bio-social characteristics, and the multi-faceted aspects of the work situation. Different work orientations will have different implications for attitudes towards participation, that is for propensity to participation. The technological and organisational features of any one plant, as well as the distribution of resources of power and authority, are part of the conditions which encourage or impede participation and the pursuit of related objectives (that is, of participatory potential). But outside the individual plant the organisation and distribution of workers within the market or segments of the labour market also affects their possibilities for participation. Finally, we need to be aware that workers' attitudes towards and potential for participation can be affected by influences beyond the workplace and community, and analysis must also take account of the fact that workers respond to wider political and economic movements. We saw for example in an earlier chapter how pressure for participation has come in waves which were associated more broadly with periods of industrial militancy and movements in the economic cycle. The period from the mid-sixties onwards produced one such wave.

The data on worker orientations is however relatively limited, both in relation to the periods when it was collected (mostly the mid-sixties to mid-seventies), the scope of the studies conducted and the groups covered. The data on attitudes towards participation is even more limited and has on the whole not been conceptualised within the wider framework of work orientations. A number of broad conclusions nevertheless seem possible. The data suggest that most workers have an instrumental orientation towards work. Related to that, the area where there is most desire for participation in decision-making (and also where it is felt there is most participation) is that of pay. The view that collective bargaining is the most effective mechanism for participation fits within that context. Brown et al. (1983) have noted however that an instrumental attitude towards work does not exclude an interest in other aspects of the job. This is consonant with the generally expressed wish for an increase in participation, strongly focused on areas related to the organisation and conditions of work rather than on the wider authority structure of the enterprise.

Beyond this the picture is less clear. Workers who emphasise the intrinsic elements of work will necessarily have a positive attitude towards participation at the level of task and work organisation. The material from BSC might be read as indicating that the less task alienation there is the more demand there is for higher level participation, at least for manual workers. It might also indicate that the more institutional forms of participation there are (in the case of BSC collective bargaining, worker directors and joint consultation) the more demand there is for higher level participation. Either way it suggests that the appetite for participation is related to experience of it. This is borne out by the material on shop stewards which shows that they tend to want more participation than their members, in the sense of a greater degree of joint decision-making, although in areas which are still at the socio-technical rather than the political level of the organisation.

The data on attitudes towards participation tends to be drawn from workers who, broadly speaking, are in the primary segments of the labour market. These are located in enterprises which provide the greatest potential for participation. Within the secondary segments people are gathered who, both in terms of their personal characteristics and of the social situation they inhabit, will have little cohesion and little stability. Organisation, knowledge and understanding, important underpinnings of participation, are difficult to achieve in such situations. Potential is low. However, even in the primary segments with strong potential and at a time of high public interest, the data indicates that whilst there was a general demand for increased participation, there was also a general acceptance of the existing authority structure of the enterprise. Despite some signs of a cultural change, with a heightening of expectations, particularly amongst younger workers, the data appears to suggest that most workers are uninterested in participating in their work organisations other than in relatively limited ways at the socio-technical level. Their values represent no basic challenge to managerial authority.

Further Reading
Rose (1975) provides a valuable account of the development of theorising about worker attitudes and behaviour. Blackburn and Mann (1979), and Brown et al. (1983) offer overviews of empirical material on work orientations. Gordon (1972), Edwards et al. (1975), Loveridge and Mok (1979) and Wilkinson (1980) present material on labour market dualism and labour market segmentation. In addition to Loveridge et al. (1983), Marchington (1980), Heller et al. (1979) and Brannen et al. (1976), other material on worker attitudes to participation can be found in Ramsay (1976), and Hespe and Wall (1976); and on local full-time union officials' attitudes towards participation, in Dowling et al. (1981).

5 · Management Organisation and Attitude

As we saw in the first chapter, the growth of the modern industrial economy, for Weber, was based on bureaucratic organisation in which roles were filled on merit, and administration was conducted through the use of elaborate and precise rules and procedures. Supervisors were obeyed because subordinates accepted the rational-legal basis of their authority. The formal rationality of organisations was essential to the development of capitalism. Administration must be appropriated for capitalism to be effective. We have seen that historically management has been less than enthusiastic about any form of participation. The philosophy of private enterprise and the high value placed on formal market efficiency and a structure of hierarchic authority are likely to incline them in this direction. Weber also acknowledged, however, the likely conflict between the procedures designed to observe formal rationality and other sets of social values and goals. In this chapter we consider both structural and normative pressures within the system of production which might modify a formally rational approach to industrial administration; we also look at management orientations towards worker participation.

It is important to remember too that pressures on management may arise from changes in the broader political and cultural systems. Despite a laissez faire ideology, government in the nineteenth century was increasingly forced to legislate on the legal position of unions as organisations. The growth of trade unions and their legitimisation by the State acted as a general constraint on the exercise of unilateral power by management. The State itself played little role in shaping the nature of the relationships between workers and employers, except in a limited number of areas related to health, safety and the protection of vulnerable groups, and in times of war (Clegg, 1980). The tradition of voluntarism began to change after the second world war; particularly in the last two decades, as we have seen in Chapter Three, the State has elaborated a series of individual and collective rights for labour which, in purely formal terms, modifies managerial authority and power and constrains management's relationship with labour. In addition the possibility of boardroom and other aspects of participation, as a result either of internal political initiatives or of external pressure from the European Community, has presented a threat to managerial authority. It might be expected that these developments of industrial citizenship would generate both specific and general cultural pressure on management to modify its attitudes and behaviour towards labour, that is to affect market behaviour towards labour as commodity.

Within the industrial system there have been a number of structural changes which, it might be argued, affect management's susceptibility to workers' participation. Technology, which Marx saw as having a determining role in the social relationships of production, is seen by some writers as evolving in a way which will increasingly make management more amenable to some forms (usually socio-technical) of participation. The increasing scale of industrial, commercial and service operations and the divorce, if not between ownership and ultimate control at least between majority ownership and general management, might also be seen to affect the organisational potential for participation. For example, the resultant professionalisation of management and associated trend towards achievement-, rather than status-oriented management, particularly in increasingly bureaucraticized and technologically complex organisations, might be seen to facilitate participation. Alternatively, the increasing divorce of ownership and control, along with increased State aid, support and involvement for industry which we saw in Chapter Three, might be seen to undermine the validity of market-related notions of efficiency. We go on to consider these arguments and then look at recent evidence on management's attitudes towards participation.

Technological change

The development of different types of technology has been perceived as having a variety of effects on the managerial role. A number of writers have broadly categorised technological systems into craft or unit production, mass production and process production, and have suggested that different types of production system are related to different patterns of management organisation and control (Woodward, 1965; Blauner, 1967; Perrow, 1970). Within craft production there is a minimal management co-ordinating role and freedom for innovation and problem discussion and solution at the point of production. Certain features of craft production were retained within some forms of large scale industry, for example shipbuilding. Such industries have been characterised by Stinchcombe as having a system of craft administration (Stinchcombe, 1959). By this he means that they have a relatively shallow management pyramid; many of the detailed decisions as to what standard tasks are carried out, and how, are undertaken by workers whose craft training socialises them into technical and occupational competence. Within such industries workers exercise a high degree of control, not only over their tasks but often also over manpower issues such as manning and recruitment (Brown and Brannen, 1970).

Within mass production industry, by contrast, the management function is elaborated. Mass production enterprises have long product runs, production processes are centrally designed, and efficiency is gained by breaking down tasks into short repetitive cycles. There is a growth of administrative and specialist staff who take over control of the design and planning of work, the organisational strategy, and the planning and execution of manpower and employment matters. For writers such as Braverman the separation of control from execution typifies modern industry. 'The physical processes of production are now carried out more or less blindly, not only by the workers who perform them but often by lower ranks of supervisory employees as well. Production units operate like a hand, worked, corrected and controlled by a distant brain.' (Braverman, 1974, p. 125). The numbers and specialisms of management increase to handle the co-ordination and flow of work; at the same time the personnel and industrial relations functions grow to deal, respectively, with problems arising from lack of motivation and with conflict (ibid.).

The development of mass production industry has been paralleled by the growth of scientific management and its associated techniques, and by the development of a complex and bureaucratic division of labour with management. However, as we saw in Chapter One, it is possible to criticise Braverman's analysis for its lack of recognition of the forces of worker resistance to management control; it can also be criticised for its deterministic view of management strategies. Friedman, for example, has argued that in addition to the 'direct control' strategies implied in scientific management, it is also possible to identify a continuation of practices involving delegation of control along occupational lines. This strategy of 'responsible autonomy' involves giving particular groups of workers autonomy and responsibility for particular areas of work. Its adoption is not, for Friedman, directly linked to the technological system but rather to the importance of particular groups of workers to the profitability of the business. This importance may spring from the effectiveness of their collective organisation, or from their particular skills, or the degree of their centrality to the production process (Friedman, 1977).

Other writers, whilst sharing in outline Braverman's analysis of mass production industry, do not see it as typifying the trend. They suggest, as we have seen, that with the development of process production there is a change in the nature of the control function. Blauner for example argued that process production restores worker control over the work process, and meaning to work. In a highly automated plant the worker takes back from management the duty of supervising the quality of work, and relationships between management and worker are based on consultation and communication rather than command (Blauner, 1967). Similarly Touraine argued that in process production the involvement of the worker with his job is dependent on 'the psychology of management, supervision and workers, that is to say on the state of human and industrial relations which are in turn social and organisation factors' (Touraine, 1962). Similarly the work of both Woodward and Perrow suggested that enterprises with process production had more flexible organisation, a greater degree of delegation of authority and a more permissive management system. Because the control system is improved and built into the technology, management and supervisors are spared the police function. Hierarchical control becomes less important (Woodward, 1965; Perrow, 1970).

Mallet provided a slightly different gloss on the implications of technology (Mallet, 1975). He suggested that the sub-division and deskilling of labour in mass production meant that labour was a variable cost which could be allowed to fluctuate with the state of the market. With process production labour becomes a fixed cost. Labour possesses a detailed knowledge and expertise in particular complex machinery. This is derived from costly in-plant training and produces types of skill that are plant-specific and difficult to find on the open market. Management, therefore, needs to hang on to its labour and labour has skills which only have value in specific enterprises. Management and workforce are, therefore, locked together in a process of mutual indispensability. 'The essential element of production having become its equipment, the essential concern of the capitalist will be to amortise exceedingly costly machinery in the minimum time period and he will naturally seek to adjust his labour and investment policies. The problem which presents itself for him will no longer be as in 1925 or 1935, to have at hand a flexible and easily "condensible" reservoir of labor but on the contrary to assure himself a permanent workforce trained in the particular techniques of the company.' (Mallet, 1975, p. 40). Whilst, as we have noted in Chapter One, the implications of Blauner and Woodward's analyses are different from those of Mallet in relation to the integration of the worker into the enterprise, the implications for management strategy and organisation in relation to labour appear to be the same. Scientific management gives way to strategies based on human relations and employee welfare considerations.

The implications of technology for the management and control structures of the enterprise are more open than this literature suggests. The work of Trist and others at the Tavistock Institute has demonstrated that there is considerable scope for choice in the design of a social system to operate a particular technology (Trist et al., 1963). More recently Gallie has suggested in a comparative study of oil refineries in France and Britain that management styles and strategies were different, even in factories in which the production systems were similar. In the French refineries managerial power within the factory remained formally absolute; worker representatives had no rights of effective control over decision making. A form of paternalism led to generous encouragement of welfare and social activities but exclusion from any effective say in issues of work organisation. British management by contrast operated a 'semi-constitutional strategy and sought to ensure effective performance by obtaining the explicit consent of the workforce to rules governing work organisation and terms of employment' (Gallie, 1979, p. 302). More broadly, as Poole has pointed out, in countries at similar stages of technical development radically different types of institutional arrangements for handling relations between workers and management have evolved (Poole, 1981). At the beginning of this chapter we noted the role of the State as an influence on management behaviour and in earlier chapters made the point that over time the state of the market has some importance. Whilst in a broad sense the technological system constrains or determines the social organisation of production it is clear that it does not do so in any direct way. It seems more likely that technology acts as one amongst a variety of contextual factors affecting management orientation to participation and that its effects are mediated through a variety of market, organisational and general cultural factors.

The social composition of management

The process of industrialisation has involved a movement away from the individual entrepreneur as manager, towards complex management systems with a multiplicity of roles and functions, leading in turn to the rise of professional managements. There has also been a related separation of ownership from managerial control. The general evidence is that management as a social stratum has grown over the course of the century, whereas owners have declined in numbers. The 1971 census estimated that about 1.8 million people in Britain occupied managerial jobs; this accounted for 6.2% of employment; in 1911 management accounted for 3.3% of employment. Over the same period employers declined from 4.6% of the economically active population to 1.9%. In the period up to 1981 this trend has continued. In a study of class formation and social stability Heath argues that the concentration of industry and the spread of large-scale bureaucracies have undoubtedly squeezed out the individual entrepreneur (Heath, 1981). In an illustration from the steel industry, he describes how in 1865 56% of steel manufacturers were 'independents', men who had founded the firm which they controlled, 30% were heirs and only 14% were salaried professionals or administrators. By 1953 the 'independents' were down to 3%, the administrators up to 57%, but the heirs had more than held their own, comprising 40% of the total; Heath concludes that bureaucracy has triumphed over the self-made man but that in the boardroom the family has retained its position: 'bureaucracy has replaced the market not the family' (p. 95).

It has been argued that these developments have produced a new social grouping, separate and with different interests from those who own industry (Berle and Means, 1932). Its formation has been encouraged by the increasing scale and technical complexity of industry, requiring an educated and technically and administratively sophisticated management. Studies of British managers indicate that men with higher educational qualifications are today well represented in managerial positions. The proportion of managers with degrees has risen more quickly than the proportion of graduates in the population as a whole (Parker et al., 1980, p. 114). Management has also developed its own institutions and a body of knowledge labelled 'management thought', which has both a technical and a legitimatory function. 'The legitimatory function was primarily linked to the securing of social recognition and approval for managerial authority and the way in which it was used, while the technical function was primarily linked to the search for practical means of rendering that authority maximally effective.' (Child, 1969, p. 23). This thesis of 'managerialism' suggests that managers develop common interests and a common social identity distinct from that of owners, and that they are likely to run businesses in a way that emphasises organisational survival rather than profit. It is inferred from this that the nature of the relationship between management and the workforce will be modified; that there will be increased recognition by managers of joint interests and that they will be more open to issues of participation than industrial owners whose prime orientation is profit.

The thesis has been criticised, however, at a number of levels. Changes in the composition of ownership do not necessarily mean that the holders of managerial positions perform their functions to achieve different ends. Indeed Pahl and Winkler have suggested that professional managers are more capable of achieving and more orientated to profit than owner managers (Pahl and Winkler, 1974). Moreover, the similarity of goals between senior managers, share owners, financiers, and other elite groups is reinforced through the interlocking of directorships and the personal share ownerships of senior managers (Stansworth and Giddens, 1974). Other evidence suggests that senior managers are socially and normatively integrated with industrial owners. In examining data collected in the 1972 Oxford Study of Social Mobility, Heath points out that three quarters of the men in social class 1 (higher grade professionals, administrators and managers and large proprietors) had come from lower social classes. However, within that grouping over half the managers had come from working class origins as opposed to only one quarter of proprietors (Heath, 1981). He then went on to examine whether, despite different class backgrounds, those in a common economic position 'are also involved in a common web of social relationships, sharing common attitudes and values' (p. 228).

Taking friendship patterns as indicating relational aspects, and voting patterns normative aspects of behaviour Heath concludes that the friendship of men in social class 1 is more narrowly circumscribed than their kinship connections and that there is greater political homogeneity than in other classes. Whilst class 1 is quite heterogeneous in its membership (40% coming from blue collar homes) it is more homogeneous in its friendship and voting patterns than other classes; upward mobility replenishes the talent of the dominant class without unduly undermining its cohesion and potential for communal action to further its interests. A proportion of the upwardly mobile do not however assimilate, and retain normative allegiance to their lower class background (Heath, 1981). We shall see later in the chapter that the voting behaviour of managers is a good indicator of their attitudes to worker participation.

In reviewing the literature on the relationships between owners and managers one author has concluded: 'When all the evidence on the concentration of wealth and the social connections between owners of wealth and those involved in managing the organisations which create wealth is taken into account, and this is put alongside the fact that the rewards accruing to senior managers (in the form of salaries, bonus, fringe benefits, dividend on their own shares, and personal prestige) relate to their performance with regard to wealth creation, we can see that any claims that organisations are run in the interests of a dominant social class are well founded.' (Watson, 1980, p. 204). All of this suggests that the thesis defining management as different and with separate interests from owners is dubious, and that nothing should be inferred from the development of management as a category about the distinctiveness of their interests or orientation, in relation to the owners of organisations. Nevertheless, within management there are a number of factors operating which are likely to create a diversity of interests and orientations.

Organisational diversity

We examined earlier the relationships that have been posited between technology, management structure and management orientation. The size of an organisation will clearly also affect the structure and division of labour within management. We have noted in Chapter Three the long term trend towards company growth and concentration within the British economy. As companies grow in size they begin to make use of routinised procedures and to develop more specialised management. In addition the spatial development of companies over a number of geographical areas, as well as product diversification, leads them to adopt multi-divisional structures with a variety of sets of control relationships between head office, divisional headquarters, and plants or other establishments (Chandler, 1962).

Within a large company orientation can vary significantly between senior managers and head office functions and those who overlook branch factories and departments. Even within senior management, whilst there may be certain common assumptions about basic economic objectives there are likely to be different views about the means of achieving these. One study of senior managers found that attitudes towards issues such as variety in the work environment, risk taking, and approaches to problem solving varied as between managers in charge of different functional areas. Financial managers and quality control managers tended to be least flexible and most conservative; research, personnel and marketing managers tended to exhibit the greatest flexibility (Ellis and Child, 1973). In part these differences can be explained in relation to the different roles performed by these groups within the grading system of the organisation. Differences in attitude may also reflect the influence of prior occupational socialisation and of continued contact with external reference groups. 'The presence of different groups within management, each sharing a separate identity based on common social origins, career, status and occupational position, points to the fact that management is not homogeneous or clearly identifiable.' (Parker et al., 1980, p. 124).

Batstone suggests that within companies the room for lower level bodies to develop their own policies is limited; they must operate within guidelines and procedures set by the headquarters offices. Within head offices a variety of experts, divorced in skill, location and background from those in operating units, play a key role in the elaboration of procedures and the formulation of general policy. Moreover, strategic decisions are based less on the performance of individual operating units than upon how key members of the general office conceive the overall interests of the company. 'Conflicts of interest are therefore likely and lower levels of the organisation will often seek to manipulate procedures and attempt to create room for independent action.' (Batstone, 1979, p. 260).

The presence of different groups within management, with different orientations towards their roles, suggests that a simple Weberian rationality model is inadequate as a basis for understanding management. Burns has suggested that organisations can be decomposed into three separate but related elements; the working system, the political system, and the career structure (Burns, 1969). The working system represents the total membership of the concern brought together to achieve the working aims of the organisation. The systematic exploitation of the membership resources of the organisation in order to realise its ends has been conceived traditionally in terms of bureaucracy, but such a view of organisations is, Burns argues, intellectually and time bound. Mechanistic systems of control find themselves in difficulty in times of change and instability. His research led him to ask why in the face of market and technical changes organisations did not move from a mechanistic to a more appropriate organic form of control. His answer was that the commitment of the individual to a concern was not limited to those commitments which 'enlist him as a resource in a working organisation. In addition he is a member of a group or section with sectional interests in conflict with those of other groups or sections, and he is also one individual among many to whom the position they occupy, relative to others, and their future security or betterment, are matters of deep concern.' (p. 246). The organisation, Burns was arguing, is not just one means-ends system, but represents several means-end systems for realising the goals of individuals. Any concern will contain these three systems. 'All three will act and react upon the others.' (p. 247).

The consequences of diversity in management orientations, and of management's being a political and career-oriented system, for its attitudes and behaviour in relation to worker participation, are not addressed directly in this literature. Burns's analysis would suggest however that management's political and career interests in organisations might lead it to resist the development of worker participation even if the needs of the working system might demand it. In similar vein Batstone has argued that the development of particular forms of expertise amongst management, even those related to the management of labour, does not simply respond to the needs of the work organisation: it is deeply impregnated by the political and career elements of organisational behaviour and is likely to be antipathetic to the extension of participation (Batstone, 1979). He suggests that such development reflects, at least in part, the purposes of those who are in a position to sponsor and control the pursuit of knowledge, their particular priorities and the existence of a hierarchical structure. Whilst experts develop values of their own these are not necessarily in contra-distinction to the primary goals of employers. Industrial experts are encapsulated within and tend to accept wider organisational constraints. The claim to expertise is in part related to the political system within the enterprise.

Batstone notes that claims to expertise correspond to some extent with an ability to enforce a certain exclusivity. 'The claim to expertise is largely a political exercise aimed at improving security status and other rewards.' (p. 254). He also points out that experts are often managers with their own hierarchy. At the top of these hierarchies the people selected are picked not so much on the basis of their professional skills as on their readiness to accommodate the assumptions of the dominant management team. They are 'trusted brokers' (p. 255). Whilst professional groups such as personnel managers may wish to promote participation (including collective bargaining) this is likely to be within parameters which are consonant with the general goals of management in the enterprise. Following this analysis the extension of participation (through, for example, developments in labour law) might lead to the extension of power for the personnel experts rather than the sharing of power between all groups in the enterprise.

It is important to emphasise however that models of formal rationality, based on financial and market calculations, are a continuing and indeed dominant framework within the enterprise. As we noted earlier, the evidence does not suggest that the interests of management as a category are likely to be different from those of owners. At the corporate level of the enterprise senior managers are integrated into the broader business community. The financial and market position of the firm is the dominant interest and area of activity of boards of directors, even where these play a relatively passive role in the direction of the enterprise (Gordon, 1965; Knight, 1979; see also Chapter Six). Market competition is a prime motivator of and constraint on management behaviour (Nichols, 1969). Within the organisation accounting procedures and the evolving profession of accountancy have provided an important institutional expression of formal rationality. Batstone points out that accounting systems do not simply record aspects of company performance. They are a key feature of organisational procedures and as such lay down the terms of legitimate debate within the organisation; as they have evolved they have given primacy to capital rather than labour. He argues that accounting systems operate as 'vocabularies of motive'. They 'reflect the priorities of the dominant groups and indicate to more junior managers the way in which they are expected to behave . . . . Achievement of plans and targets is its own legitimation and generally management attempt to do exactly that. Where they feel they cannot do so they often attempt, by manipulation or other means, to provide accounts of their actions in terms of the dominant vocabulary of motive.' (Batstone, 1979, p. 258). It is also the case at a more general level that accounting vocabularies fix the terms of argument under which debates between employees and management, over such issues as pay or rationalisation and redundancy, take place.

Management attitudes towards participation

Studies of management which stress its diversity largely ignore its relations with the work force, while those of worker participation tend to treat management in a relatively homogeneous way. All social groupings have forces acting on them which tend to fragment them and others which tend to unify them. The sociological problem is to identify which are the salient forces in relation to particular forms of social action. In this section we consider a number of studies of management attitudes towards participation which have been conducted over the last decade. It will be remembered that the period saw considerable public emphasis on the issue of worker participation.

We turn first to a study of worker participation conducted in the British Steel Corporation in the early 1970s. At that time, although the steel industry had been recently nationalised, the majority of management had spent most of their working lives in the private sector. As a corporate entity BSC had a positive policy towards worker participation, it had introduced worker directors onto its divisional boards, was developing an organisation-wide structure of joint consultation, and had an elaborate system of collective bargaining. In the course of the study, all members of the divisional boards of the Corporation were interviewed as well as a sample of plant managers (Brannen et al., 1976).

The authors found that management thinking about participation was related to a number of frames of reference. The first of these was based on notions of efficiency and profit. Another related to hierarchy and expertise. Managers were sensitive about their authority status; they believed that management had a right to manage which stemmed from their role as agents of the owners (whether the State or private individuals and institutions) and from their expertise. A further framework related to worker satisfaction and worker rights. One (though rather weak) element in this was the notion of industrial suffrage; another the frustrations created by the workers' subordinate position within the industrial enterprise, and the nature of the tasks to be performed.

These frames of reference were related to another based on certain images of relationships in industry.* Some managers saw these as unitary and

*For a general discussion of management frames of reference and industrial relations see Fox, 1974, pp. 248-96.

stressed harmony and co-operation between managers and workers as both desirable and endemic. Managers holding to a unitary framework tended to place strong emphasis on managerial rights and the necessity for hierarchy as a means to efficiency. They rejected any notion of industrial suffrage but were willing to encourage limited forms of participation in terms of increasing communication, satisfaction and teamwork. Other managers saw industrial relationships as essentially dichotomous, with workers having no legitimate interests in the organisation other than offering their labour power in return for a wage. Such managers also placed a strong stress on hierarchy and on efficiency. They rejected the view that participation might increase efficiency or that the workforce has any rights in the company other than as labour. Finally, some managers held a pluralistic view of worker-management relations; they recognised several sets of legitimate and differing relationships in the firm, and saw a variety of contracts and compromises as a natural and essential element of organisational behaviour. They also emphasised hierarchy, but saw participation as a way of balancing interests, acknowledging workers' rights and enhancing efficiency.

The authors suggest that different frameworks are drawn on in different contexts. They indicate the variety of factors which inform managers' approaches to participation. However, when asked directly which was the most important reason for participation the majority of managers placed considerations of efficiency above increasing either job satisfaction or workers' rights to have some say in decision-making. The logic of the managerial view of participation emerged most clearly in answers to questions about what they understood by participation and the areas they considered appropriate for it. For most directors and managers participation was about workers making their views known to management, and receiving information from management. Managers tended to emphasise the reciprocity of information exchange more than directors. Directors, on the other hand, were willing to see this form of participation take place over a wide range of areas, from welfare activities to company development plans. Managers were less willing to accept participation in corporate issues. This may be because directors had reached the top of their career, and were secure in their authority; participation was about keeping management/ worker relationships harmonious. It did not impinge on them directly. For managers, especially more junior managers, 'to allow participation, particularly in areas of major importance, would be a threat to their authority and to their sense of professionalism. Further, consultation and discussion take time and they saw it as inefficient, particularly in areas where the only important dimensions of the decision were technical, that is related to management and production.' (p. 49).

The data concerning management views on participation in the British Steel Industry was collected in 1970 within a traditional heavy manufacturing industry which had been newly nationalised. Other studies conducted subsequently in other industries and as general surveys over the whole of industry have tended broadly to confirm and elaborate this analysis. In a national survey of companies in the private sector employing more than 200 people, conducted in 1976, interviews were held with a number of directors and plant managers in each company (Knight, 1979). When asked what participation should involve the model response for directors was 'discussion with the workforce before management made decisions'. Less than one-fifth felt it ought to involve any form of joint decision-making. For managers at plant level the pattern was more varied. Both the senior plant manager and the manager responsible for the largest white collar group of workers mirrored the pattern of response at board level. But over one-third of senior production management felt that participation should involve joint decision-making and half of personnel management defined it in this way. As in the Steel Corporation data however, this picture is modified if one looks at the areas which various management respondents felt were appropriate for participation.

The survey found very little support amongst either directors or managers for participation in the area of capital investment; increased support, but still at a low level, for participation in production methods, strong support for participation in welfare matterrs and intermediate support on pay and disciplinary matters (Tables 56, 58, 40D and 48D). In other words, where traditionally there are collectively bargained agreements as over pay or discipline then management tend to accept joint decision-making; likewise in areas which are peripheral to business such as welfare. But in central areas of management prerogative management are unwilling to accept participation. We can also see from this material that within the general parameters of managerial consensus there is some variation of attitude according to role held. The report gives no breakdown on variation in attitude by either size or sector.

Marchington presents similar findings in his study of 'Kitchenco', a medium-size manufacturing firm (Marchington, 1980). He found broad acceptance by most managers in the firm of the notion of worker participation but states that 'it is viewed in a relatively limited manner; that is participation should not upset current systems of decision-making and company objectives but should be integrated into the framework so as to provide more opportunity for employee opinions to be taken into acount.' (p. 101). The major reason for most managers wishing to support participation was to increase efficiency. Participation was seen largely as being concerned with consultation and information flow. Management were unwilling to allow participation on pricing and new product policies, were willing to consult on recruitment and to a greater extent on redundancies and to negotiate on pay (p.103).

Marchington sets out a series of problems which management had with the notion of participation. 'During the course of the interviews managers regularly referred to their superior ability in decision-making, to their ability to be more objective than stewards could be when it came to choosing a course of action, and generally holding a wider range of knowledge and information' (p. 108). He argues that defence of this prerogative is more pronounced if it is felt to be in a particularly crucial area of the business. Conversely, the less important the situation the more willing management may be to share control. The second problem seen by managers is the inability of employees to contribute to effective decision-making. This is seen as both a problem of ability (if they had the ability they would be managers already) or of training. He points out however that 'there is rarely any consideration of the possible effects that training may have on stewards' acceptance and maintenance of the status quo' (p. 109). The third problem area is that the introduction of particular schemes of participation is seen by some members of the management team as undermining their position. At Kitchenco this was the case with the foremen. 'For the foremen in particular the system appears to create a feeling of "lost" control and it is probably for this reason that the degree of participation at Kitchenco is in excess of what they feel it ought to be.' (p. 112).

Cressey and his colleagues carried out a survey of 48 Scottish enterprises in 1978, which in part replicated the study conducted by Knight but included construction and service industries as well as the manufacturing sector. (Cressey et al., 1981). To try to establish some context for investigating attitudes towards worker participation during the public discussion of the topic at the time of the Bullock enquiry they first asked respondents if they had ever discussed participation in their enterprise. The results were interesting. It was only amongst managing directors that the majority (62%) had had formal discussions in the enterprise and where another 17% had discussed it informally. Just under half of the personnel managers had discussed participation formally but another 25% had had informal discussions. In contrast only 42% of line managers had ever talked about the topic either formally or informally. This pattern of results was attributed to 'senior management anticipating and reacting to the prospect of legislation' (p. 25). Also, 'in about a quarter of the enterprises in the survey industrial democracy and participation appeared to be a live topic irrespective of the anticipation of legislation....Managers saw these discussions as being primarily concerned with participative involvement and communication rather than "industrial democracy" as such and tended to be concerned with what were matters appropriate to consultative discussion or negotiation and how the group could be managed in a more participatory style, taking this not necessarily as an end in itself, but rather as a means to greater efficiency, flexibility or more harmonious industrial relations.' (ibid.).

Seventy-nine per cent of managers favoured participation as a general idea. However, when discussing specific participative ideas there was a much lower level of support. Managers saw participation as having two main roles. The first was educational; through participation management would be able to inform the workforce 'where the company stood, the market problems it faced, its performance over the current period and the role of each plant and section of the workforce in that performance. The purpose of such communication was usually to encourage realism in the workforce's attitudes and a greater commitment to the fortunes of the company.' (p. 48). The second role was the reverse of this, ensuring that shop floor knowledge and attitudes were available to management for its decision-making processes. Senior managers were more likely than junior managers to support participation; junior managers were more likely to see the problems involved. Most managers stressed however that 'participation, of whatever sort, had to be advisory. It was complementary to management's right to manage and make decisions, not a challenge to that or a diminution of it.' (p. 50).

The final study we turn to is a national sample survey of 185 managers carried out in 1977, by means of a self-completion postal questionnaire (Clegg et al., 1978). The authors found that a majority of managers (73%) expressed themselves in favour of participation; most of those in favour, however, were interested in 'soft' approaches to participation (that is forms of direct participation related to tasks and work groups) rather than 'hard' approaches (that is, based on indirect representation as in collective bargaining or worker director schemes). Those against any form of participation (27% of the sample) were all politically to the right (based on a self-rating of position as right, centre right, centre left or left), and opposed to sharing control with their workforce, even over the organisation of the worker's own job. They thought that industrial democracy was an irrelevant pipe dream. People only work for money. In terms of the real needs of British industry, profit incentives, management incentives and investment incentives were the real issues. Clegg and his colleagues felt that this group 'came closest to holding a dichotomous perspective' (p. 13).

Those managers favouring 'soft' approaches to participation (34% of the sample) tended to be politically right but more centre right than the previous subset; they thought participation was largely a side issue, but an essential one. They felt that employees should be consulted over the organisation of their own jobs and associated issues. A typical view was: 'the workers themselves must become more involved in order that they can be more aware of their own responsibilities and contribute their know-how to the efficient running of the firm.' (p. 15). The authors interpret the dominant frame of reference of this group as unitary.

Very few managers in the sample were in favour of 'hard' forms of participation alone; but just over a third of the sample favoured a combination of 'soft' and 'hard' approaches to participation. This group contained most of the politically left managers, as well as some of those on the right. The majority favoured sharing power and responsibility more democratically with employees and felt that industrial democracy was essential. A typical view was that 'industrial democracy should be concerned predominantly with joint decision-making on nearly all aspects of an industrial concern' (p. 15). The authors note that 'while the perspectives held in this group cannot by any means be described as radical, there is considerable support for real changes in the extent of employee involvement in decision making.' (ibid.). Extending the range of decision-making covered by collective bargaining is seen as the best means forward for 'hard' participation by this group. Although the authors do not label this group it approximates to the pluralist perspective.

Clegg and his colleagues conclude that attitudes to participation in their sample were importantly related to political orientation; they also note that managers in the manufacturing sector were more knowledgeable about participation than those outside manufacturing and that the more knowledgeable managers were also those who were most optimistic about industrial democracy (p. 12). 'Soft' forms of participation were seen as increasing efficiency, reducing conflict and increasing employee satisfaction; they were popular amongst most managers and seen as furthering the aims of managers and workers (but not trade unions). 'Hard' forms of participation were less popular and seen as furthering only the aims of workers and unions. They were seen as being about power and 72% of the sample agreed with the proposition that 'in the final analysis industrial democracy is about power.' The authors conclude that 'many managers expect a number of potentially highly pragmatic benefits to flow from the direct forms whilst acknowledging (rather ruefully) that the debate and practice of industrial democracy revolves around the issue of power' (p. 10).

Conclusion

We have considered in this chapter a series of structural factors that might affect the orientation of managers towards participation; we have also looked at some recent data on orientations. No clear view emerged from the literature as to how technological and organisational change, and the increasing complexity and professionalisation of management organisation are likely to affect management attitude and behaviour in relation to worker participation. Our consideration of a number of studies of management attitudes towards participation does not suggest that these factors are of primary importance.

All the surveys on management's orientation towards participation we have discussed in the previous pages took place during the 1970s, a period when there was a resurgence of interest in society at large in the issue of participation. There are a number of common threads in management views. Most managers expressed interest in the idea of participation. Few managers defined participation in terms of sharing the decision-making process with the workforce. For most managers across industry and across managerial occupations participation was about communication and consultation, a means of involving the workforce and increasing their commitment in order to increase efficiency. These are the major elements of management's orientation. Within that however there are a number of variations. Those with a 'left' political persuasion are more positively oriented towards participation than those of the 'right'. Those with a professional interest in the management of discontent, personnel and industrial relations managers, show a more positive orientation than those of their line management peers, and senior managers and directors show more interest and feel less threatened than junior managers. There is some variation therefore, on occupational and ideological lines. There is also some broad variation by industrial sector, with manufacturing industry showing more positive attitudes than the service sector and the public sector more positive attitudes than the private.

It is important to emphasise that the data on variations within management is thin. What comes across most strikingly is the homogeneity of management attitudes across occupational and organisational boundaries, and their deep commitment to existing organisational structures and managerial prerogatives. Thus, one can conclude that even at a time of great public interest in the issue of worker participation there was little pressure from within management for an extension of participation other than of a kind which did not affect the authority structure. There was however some reaction to external pressure. That most managers expressed interest in participation might be seen as a reflection of this. It is also the case that where external forces led to the creation of participative institutions management tended to accommodate to these. Thus the joint determination of pay and conditions through collective bargaining is accepted; and where there are elaborate systems of participation, as in the nationalised industries, experience and knowledge lead also to a degree of acceptance.

Most studies of management attitudes towards participation have not built in factors such as size, technology, market situation, ownership, or management organisation as independent variables. On the evidence brought together in this chapter it is possible to suggest that the effect of these variables is likely to be indirect rather than direct; that is, they may be more important in producing a worker response, or a political or cultural response to which management must react. Management practice and indeed, management thought, in the areas of participation, might best be understood as reflecting the self-assertion of labour at workplace, company and societal level.* Participation is considered by management only when there are threats to managerial authority, and paradoxically in order to maintain it.

*For an elaboration of this perspective in the context of a critique of management science see Wood and Kelly, 1978.

Further Reading

Poole and Mansfield (1980) provide a useful set of essays on management's role in industrial relations. Abrahamsson (1979) sets out in brief form much of the classical and current literature on bureaucracy and the administration of organisations and explores the possibilities of organisational democracy as an alternative to bureaucracy. Fox (1974b) is again a source of material on managerial strategies to gain employee compliance, on their failure and the reasons for these failures, and on the limitations on worker participation within an inegalitarian society. Child (1969) on the development of management thought, and the critique in Wood and Kelly (1978) of management science are also relevant. In addition to the material on management attitudes towards participation contained in the latter part of the chapter Elliot (1978) provides material on the public stances of management organisations. See also C.B.I. (1973 and 1979) and B.I.M. (1977).

6 · Worker Directors: an Analysis of Participation in Practice

The idea of worker directors is not new. We have seen in Chapter Two how they were introduced into a number of gas companies at the end of the nineteenth century as part of profit sharing schemes; these schemes continued right up until the second world war. In the inter-war years a further, though small, number of companies introduced worker directors, again in conjunction with profit sharing schemes. Worker directors also of course existed in co-operatives and co-ownership schemes; we shall look at these in Chapter Eight. The notion of having workers on the board of companies as employees rather than as owners or shareholders began to emerge in the United Kingdom in the late 1960s and the early 1970s for the first time. In Britain over this period the idea of worker directors became to a large extent synonymous in public discussion with that of worker participation. An analysis of both public rhetoric and actual practice serves therefore to illustrate some of the issues surrounding worker participation.

The boardroom is the formal symbol of corporate authority in both the public and private sectors of industry. The actual role of the board and its mode of operation within companies has been the subject of some debate. In this chapter we first look at some of the evidence on the role of the board and its implications for worker participation at that level. We then go on to examine the publicly expressed views of management and trade unions as they were articulated in the course of the debate over the Bullock proposals, and the attitudes of management, unions and workforce as they were explored through systematic social research over the same period. Finally we look at the way in which those worker director schemes operating in both the public and private sectors in that period worked out in practice.

The role of the board
The gradual emergence of a debate about worker representation on company boards within Britain was paralleled by a more general debate about the nature, role, composition and effectiveness of the board in the modern corporation. There are three possible models of the board's function (Brookes, 1979). First, the orthodox view of corporate policy making in which the board plays only a limited gatekeeper role, holding a watching brief over company performance, but in which direct intervention in the operational responsibilities of management is neither expected nor welcome

save under exceptional circumstances. Second, the legal model of the board-room role which, by contrast, gives extensive formal powers to the board; in this the board is responsible for protecting the interests of shareholders, and to honour this obligation it has responsibility for defining corporate goals, and for ensuring a correct allocation of human capital and material resources to pursue these goals. A third conception of the role of the board, the progressive model, sees it neither as custodian of shareholders' rights, nor as a formal rubber-stamping body, but as one which is responsible for ensuring that 'the interests of all relevant parties – that is management, consumers, employees and ultimately society at large – are taken into consideration in the establishment and implementation of corporate goals' (p. 2). The CBI, for example, argued in a publication in 1973 that 'a company, like a natural person, must be recognised as having functions, duties and moral obligations to go beyond the pursuit of profit and the specific requirements of legislation.' (CBI, 1973.)

Whilst there are a number of different views as to the formal role and responsibilities of the board there is also a variety of types of board and of modes of boardroom operation. Pahl and Winkler have distinguished between boards which exist only to conform with company law, which they term 'pro-forma' boards, and boards which actually play a role, no matter how small, in the operation of the company, which they term 'functioning' boards. They categorise the latter into non-executive boards (which contain a substantial proportion of non-executive directors who maintain a watching brief over the running the company), subsidiary boards (that is, the boards of subsidiary operating companies which include one or more members of the board of the parent company) and cabinet boards (that is, those composed largely of the heads of the various functional divisions within the organisation). In each of the three types of functioning board Pahl and Winkler suggest that senior management operate manipulative strategies in order to get proposals through; the strategy lies in controlling the amount of information and the number of options that are put to the board. They contend that manipulation is so commonplace 'that it has become the norm, the standard expectation of most of our directors (if not yet of management textbook writers and journalists) that the board collectively does not decide or even seriously discuss anything' (Pahl and Winkler, 1974, p. 109).

Brookes has examined the role of the board through data from a large scale survey of 296 companies in manufacturing industry, in the light of the work of Pahl and Winkler and the more general debate. The evidence suggests, in his view, that 'in a substantial proportion of the companies surveyed the board of directors plays an active role in corporate policy and decision making' (Brookes, 1979, p. 77). He also argued that there was little evidence of extensive manipulation of the contents and outcome of boardroom deliberations. He concluded however that the 'survey data suggests that in fulfilling their responsibilities boards were rarely influenced by considerations other than the state of the market in which their company was operating. In other words it would appear as though the majority of companies in the manufacturing sector of British industry have boards of directors which are either unwilling or unable to act progressively. This conclusion would appear to have important implications for any proposals which, if implemented, would oblige boards to change their customary practices and procedures' (p. 78). Brookes also found that alternative power centres existed in a substantial minority of the companies surveyed. These were more common in larger companies. He argues that, 'if, as the data suggests, the locus of decision-making in larger companies tends to shift away from the board towards a series of extra-boards or sub-board level committees, it follows that the instalment of worker directors on the main board of a company would not necessarily lead to an increase in the extent and scope of worker participation in corporate policy and decision making.' (p. 78).

The worker director debate

As we have seen in Chapter Three, the TUC evidence to the Donovan Commission in 1966 called for legislation to allow companies to have trade union representatives on their boards. The Donovan report itself was negative about the idea, arguing what had become the orthodox view, that membership of the board would create an intolerable conflict of interest for trade unionists and undermine their collective bargaining role (Donovan, 1968). A Labour working party also produced a report in 1967 which mentioned the notion of worker directors in the private sector, though as a distant prospect, but called for worker director experiments on the board of publicly owned companies and industries (Elliot, 1978, p. 208). Two years later in 1969 worker directors were introduced onto the divisional boards of the British Steel Corporation which had been recently re-nationalised. Almost a decade later in 1978 worker directors were introduced onto the main board of the Steel Corporation. Meanwhile in 1978 the Post Office had also introduced worker directors onto both its main and regional boards. In the mid-1970s too, a small number of worker director schemes of a variety of kinds started in private industry.

In 1975 the government set up a committee of inquiry under Lord Bullock to look at ways of introducing workers onto the boards of companies in the private sector. The interest in worker directors in Britain was part of a broader movement which saw the introduction or amendment of legislation on worker directors or broadly similar schemes in seven European countries in the years following 1970, and serious discussion about launching worker director schemes in several others (Batstone and Davies, 1976, p. 11). The influence of the Common Market was important, as we have noted in an earlier chapter. The Bullock committee argued in its report in 1977 that company boards in private sector companies with 2,000 plus employees should be single tier boards composed of an equal number of shareholders and employee representatives, plus a smaller number of independent members. This was referred to as the 2X + Y formula. The worker representatives would be chosen through the unions. The independents would be chosen by agreement between employers and unions but in the absence of agreement a procedure was set out for arbitration (Bullock, 1977). In coming to this conclusion the committee had rejected the notion that there should be a two tier board structure, as in Germany, in which employees would be represented on the supervisory board but not on the managing board.

The Bullock Committee, apart from the chairman, consisted of three industrialists, three trade unionists, and four independents; two of these were academics with trade union sympathies, one a City solicitor, and the other the Director General of Fair Trading who resigned in the course of the enquiry to become Director General of the CBI. In fact only the chairman, the trade unionists and the two academics subscribed completely to the main report of the Committee. The solicitor dissented from it with regard to the composition of the board, arguing that there was no justification for worker directors having parity with the shareholder directors. The industrialists produced a minority report making it clear that they did not feel that workers should be represented on a company board at all, but that insofar as this had to be considered then worker directors should not be placed on single tier boards. Placing workers on the sole board of companies would in their view create a conflict of interest for worker directors, bring conflict into the boardroom, create resentment against management, cause disruption to effective board working, and embarrass the worker directors themselves who would not be equipped to contribute to the majority of discussions. They suggested the creation of a supervisory board with shareholders, employees, and independents each having one-third of the seats. Employee directors should include shop floor, supervisory and managerial employees who had worked in the company for at least ten years and had experience of below board level participation systems. Employee directors should not be elected through the trade unions. Board level participation should not be introduced until companies had at least three years' experience of a company council and until there was a simple majority of employees in favour (ibid.). Whilst the employer representatives on Bullock had rejected the main proposals they had still gone further than Britain's industrial and financial establishment wished. The majority Bullock report had also gone further than many trade unionists would have wished. John Boyd of the AUEW echoed the position of both his own and other unions when he said that 'we believe that in private industry management exists to manage and unions exist to be free, unfettered independent representatives of their members, and not to be involved with Bullock suggestions' (*The Times*, 15.6.1977).

Elliot has suggested that 'there can have been few reports prepared for a government by men eminent in their own field that received such a hostile response as the Bullock report. It was attacked with one of the most vitriolic and damning campaigns ever mounted by Britain's industrialists; it was received with some embarrassment by government ministers, who found it difficult to say very much in its favour but were tied to its principles by Labour's 1974 general election manifesto; and it was absorbed by much of the trade union movement to begin with as an aberration of Jack Jones [at that time General Secretary of the Transport and General Workers Union] and one or two others which would involve them in changes of role and behaviour that they had not begun, and did not much want, to think through.' (Elliot, 1978, p. 241). The employers' organisation, the Confederation of British Industry, refused to discuss issues of parity representation, single channel representation, or the use of law to change the composition of boards in private companies. It favoured legislation encouraging companies to set up participation agreements involving consultative structures, usually separate from collective bargaining, which would promote a communication and understanding of company policy, 'making employees aware of the reasons for the decisions that affect them —which is quite different from letting them participate actively in influencing or making decisions, let alone giving an equal say.' (p. 118).

The TUC, because of disunity in the trade union movement, also drew back from the Bullock proposals. At its 1977 congress a resolution was passed, with the support of unions antagonistic to Bullock, which whilst making token nods in its direction, insisted that legislation and board representation were by no means the only way forward. It argued that there should be statutory backing for unions who wished to establish joint control of strategic planning decisions, and that parity board representation should be an option but linked to more flexible forms of joint regulation based on collective bargaining. 'Resolution 10 at the 1977 Congress was able to attract broader support by linking more explicitly traditional (voluntary collective bargaining) and novel (extension of trade union rights through back-up legislation) approaches to the achievement of trade union goals. However, the TUC failed to initiate any significant public discussion of the general principles or detailed proposals of the government White Paper, and legislation was not forthcoming in the lifetime of the 1974-79 Labour government.' (Clark et al., 1980, p. 121).

A number of enquiries across industry, which gathered data on attitudes towards boardroom participation, were conducted at the time of or after the Bullock enquiry (Knight, 1979; Dowling et al., 1981; Cressey et al., 1981). It is interesting to compare the formal and public views expressed by management and trade union organisations about Bullock with the responses of members of these categories at the level of the firm. By and large there is a high degree of correspondence. The surveys indicated that the majority of directors and managers were opposed to boardroom participation. They tended to argue that worker directors would not have the necessary expertise, that their presence on the board would hamper decision-making and lead to decisions being taken outside the boardroom, and that worker directors would suffer from role conflict and become isolated from their members. In addition some managers felt that the instant elevation of workers to the boardroom would create resentment amongst management (Dowling et al., p. 23). Those managers in favour of worker directors saw them as channels of information rather than representation. Full-time trade union officials were also opposed to worker directors. They felt that they would be incorporated into the management structure and thus prove a threat to workplace organisation and trade union power (pp. 31-3). In contrast the majority of manual union shop stewards were found to be in favour of boardroom participation, seeing it as a means of giving them more say in and more information about the way in which their companies were run. Shop stewards from white collar unions tended to be opposed (Knight, 1979, Table 49D; Cressey et al., 1981, p. 45); they saw problems of role conflict and were cynical about the ability of worker directors to exercise influence in the face of management resistance.

We ought however to point to one further study carried out in the same period that reported rather different findings. Heller and his colleagues undertook a national household sample survey of respondents in full-time employment, covering the full range of industrial sectors and plant sizes. They found that over half the senior managers in this sample and two-thirds of middle managers thought that representation of workers on the board was desirable and that over two-thirds of supervisors and three-quarters of shopfloor and clerical workers were in favour of worker directors (Heller et al., 1979).*

Worker directors in action

Worker director schemes create new organisation roles which invert traditional hierarchical forms by moving individuals from subordinate positions within the authority structure to roles within the formal locus of authority in the organisation. Such schemes consequently cut across and may prove a threat to other established organisational roles. The notion of a worker director implicitly poses issues for control and authority not only at the top and bottom of the organisation but for intervening points as well. The creation of worker director roles and the development of such roles are likely to be problematic. There may well be a variety of perspectives within

*The survey carried out by Heller and his colleagues was conducted in the community rather than the workplace and in that respect differs from the previous work reported; it also asked fewer and more straightforward questions about worker directors than the other surveys. Because of this one may be seeing in the results a reflection of the dichotomy between general social values and those that are situationally related as well as a reflection of a more superficial as opposed to a more in-depth approach to the topic. Indeed within the same research Heller and his colleagues carried out studies in 14 organisations in the manufacturing and servicing sector of British industry. They concluded from these studies that 'there is more interest in having an increase in participation over decisions related to the immediate job and work situation than there is in participation in more distant goal and policy decisions.' (Heller et al., 1979, p. 20). These findings from their plant-based studies are much more in line with other research than the findings from their community survey.

the organisation about the legitimacy of the role and what forms of social action it is appropriate for worker directors to engage in. These perspectives will be derived from general values about stratification within the enterprise and society more generally, from the micro-politics surrounding the creation of the role and the effect the role is perceived as having on the distribution of power and resources in the organisation. They will also be derived from the degree of organisational visibility the role has, and the degree and direction of change in the operation of the organisation which is seen as following from the introduction of the role.

Those appointed to be worker directors will have a view of what the role is about, which will be formed from a variety of factors, including their attitudes towards, and the values they hold about worker participation. In addition their views will also be affected by the views and behaviour of 'significant others' and through their experience in the role. In its turn the experience of worker directors will be a function of the expectations that they and others have of the role, the mobilisation of organisational resources by themselves and others to prevent or carry through various forms of action and the patterns of cooperation and conflict, of coercion and persuasion, of failure and success in pursuit of goals that ensue, the organisational structure in which the role is performed and the location of that structure within the wider systems of community, class and market. We now go on to look at a number of case studies of worker director schemes in order to focus on the dynamics of participation in the upper echelons of organisations.

Worker directors in the British Steel Corporation

Worker directors were introduced to the group boards of the newly nationalised British Steel Corporation in 1969. Three worker directors were appointed to each of the four group boards. They were appointed by the chairman of the corporation from a short list provided by the TUC, which received nominations from individual unions. The initial appointment of the worker directors was for an experimental three year period on a part-time basis, at the same salary as other non-executive directors. The worker directors were not allowed to hold formal union positions or engage in national political activities and had to guarantee that they would respect boardroom confidentiality.

The experiment within the British Steel Corporation arose from a number of causes. In a general sense there was the increasing interest in participation and industrial democracy which began in the 1960s. More directly, the chairman and personnel director of the new corporation were positively oriented to increasing worker participation in the running of the industry as one way of overcoming its manifold economic problems. At the same time a number of groups within the trade union movement saw the nationalisation of the steel industry as an opportunity to press for real power in the management of the organisation to be shared with worker representatives (Brannen et al., 1976, pp. 82-96). The role of worker director and the structure of the scheme that was drawn up were the result of a variety of pressures and goals. 'Different expectations on both the management and the union side led to different views about the structuring of the scheme, leading to a compromise between the demands of some unions for power sharing, the reluctance of other unions to be in any way involved in management decision-making, the doubts of more traditional board members about allowing any worker involvement at the highest organisational levels and the advantages liberal directors saw in this. The role was delineated in only the broadest way; its vagueness was a function of the conflicting views as to its legitimacy and purposes held by those involved in its creation.' (Brannen, 1983).

Although initially the aims, purposes, and content of the worker director scheme were confused and ambiguous the social world into which the scheme was inserted had a variety of expectations about the scheme. As we have seen in an earlier chapter most groups within the British Steel Corporation expressed support for some form of participation, but the meaning attached to the concept varied. Variations in general attitudes to participation were also reflected in attitudes towards worker directors. Initially the directors in the British Steel Corporation were hostile to the new role and saw it as redundant and illegitimate. They had largely been opposed to the nationalisation of the industry and saw the worker director scheme simply as part of the process whereby an intolerable new order was being imposed on them. However, when they were interviewed one year after the scheme had begun a majority of directors favoured the idea of worker directors. Strong support for the concept of worker directors came from shop stewards and ordinary employees who saw worker director schemes as a mechanism for ensuring that their views were represented at board level, though the stewards were critical of the specifics of the scheme. The majority of middle management were opposed to the idea of worker directors (Brannen et al., 1976, pp. 55-8).

The twelve worker directors who were originally appointed from a variety of occupations and parts of the corporation were enthusiastic about the scheme and positively committed to their new role. It was felt that the individuals should have the necessary intellectual capacity to be acceptable members of a directorial team; wide trade union and public service experience were taken as evidence for this and also as indicating familiarity with and ability to perform in committee and bureaucratic contexts. The worker directors selected were mostly older people with an average age of 55. There was originally some over-representation of white collar workers: 'a process of selection in which candidates had to be acceptable both to trade unions and management was also likely to lay value on the moderate rather than the militant, the responsible rather than the radical.' (p. 121). In general their orientation to the role stressed communication, cooperation and the exchange of ideas. They saw themselves as middlemen who would try to link together senior management, the unions and the workforce and increase both the efficiency and the degree of industrial relations harmony in the industry.

In the early days of the worker director scheme the boardroom was the main arena for activity. Initially, given the views of fellow directors about the worker director schemes, it was a hostile one. Apart from this, the introduction of any new role into a cluster of established roles provides some threat to the existing order; the latter will need to be renegotiated and the outcome of that renegotiation will in part depend on the distribution of power. Power itself is, of course, dependent on a variety of resources, not simply of numbers, but of information, language and hegemony of values. The worker directors were entering a symbolic world which belonged to the full-time directors. They had to learn the language of the boardroom, its customs, its patterns of work organisation and the rules governing this, as well as finding out what were considered appropriate modes of eating, drinking and dressing. In order to be a worker director they had to discover what it was to be a director; to understand the rules of the game in order to play. The interests which surround the role of director are different from and at points opposed to the interests bound up in the role of worker. The pressure from the social dynamic of the boardroom is to be a good board member; that is, to be a good director rather than a good worker. There are also of course pressures on the original board members to accommodate the new role and fit it within the regular board structure. Not to do so is to invite external threat to the board from those responsible for setting up the new role, and internal instability within the board itself.

In the early months of the scheme the board came to define the worker director as an expert on the shop floor view. This definition accommodated the new role to existing roles and simultaneously legitimated it and limited it. The central structuring feature of boardroom meetings related to market considerations and profitability; the formal agenda, the content of meetings and the values and assumptions underlying both were related to these features. Issues relating to labour formed only a small part of the content of board meetings, focused usually on the control costs of labour. The area in which the worker directors were experts was both limited and predefined. Boardroom meetings were also formal and to a degree ritualistic. Agenda items remained the same from meeting to meeting. The emphasis was on the presentation of information, the rational outlining of arguments for pursuing particular projects and the avoidance of conflict. The 'dominant behaviour or norms made it difficult for the worker directors to institute change other than in an overtly deviant manner. The worker directors' contribution could only be within parameters which they themselves had not laid down.' (Brannen, 1983).

The worker directors became aware at an early stage of the constraints of the board; they saw that they did not have the same informational support as full-time directors and that there were a variety of forums of discussion and decision-making outside the board. In order to exert more influence they began to seek increasing involvement in committees in other parts of the structure, to establish contact networks with a broad variety of management; 'in part they saw this as feeding back into their boardroom role, in part as establishing the worker director role as having quasi-executive functions. Paradoxically in the search to make the worker director role effective the worker directors became increasingly integrated into the management structure and the management information system. The directorial role could only be strengthened at the expense of the worker role; but the worker role could not be maintained and was not viable in a boardroom context.' (ibid.).

The initial scheme clearly had many institutional weaknesses, particularly the lack of a clear relationship between the worker directors and the trade unions in the industry. The experimental scheme was reconsidered in 1973 and made a permanent feature of the industry. A number of changes were made in order to strengthen it institutionally by involving the trade unions more in the selection process and not barring worker directors from holding trade union offices. The modified scheme allowed each union to choose its own candidates for nomination. A joint union committee selected a short list from these nominations, which was passed to a joint trade union management committee. This joint committee made a selection from the list which then went to the chairman of the BSC for ratification. It was agreed that where the joint committee was unaminous the chairman would accept its views but that he would make the final selection where there was disagreement. It was also agreed that the worker directors could hold appropriate union offices; in the period from 1973, 12 of the 17 worker directors held union offices, some of them in or close to the negotiating process. These changes meant that the worker directors could be directly linked to the trade union movement, that they were likely to be given a higher degree of legitimacy and support by the movement and that the unions might be better placed to influence their role definition and behaviour.

Throughout the period of the 1970s the BSC suffered severe market difficulties and management/union relationships came under increasing strain. This constituted an important test of the social dynamics of the scheme. An examination of evidence during the period of the 1970s suggests however that the problems highlighted in the early days of the scheme continued. The revised selection procedure, whilst involving the unions more, was still ultimately in the hands of management. Within such a system there would be little point in the union side of the joint committee's putting forward candidates who were unacceptable to management. The various stages of the selection process therefore would act as filters to produce candidates who were best suited to the directorial role. The worker directors continued to expand their activities and to sit on a wider selection of sub-board committees at national, divisional and local level. This meant that a larger amount of their time was spent with management and that there was increasing dependence on managerially defined information.

But there was also increased involvement with the trade unions and, as we have noted, a number of the worker directors held union office. In an industry suffering continuing rationalisation, closures of works and cutbacks in the workforce it might have been expected that the development of the role of the worker director as it concerned both unions and management might have led to a high degree of role strain, but few worker directors defined their situation in these terms. 'In part this can be explained by the fact that the worker directors, *qua* worker directors, were formally accountable only to the board and not to the unions. In part it can be explained in terms of the corporatist relationships which the unions have historically held with management in the steel industry in Britain; 1980 was the first national strike in that industry since 1926. In part it can be explained by the kinds of people who both select themselves and were selected to be worker directors.' (ibid.).

Naturally they saw their role in the rationalisation process of the industry as problematic. They did nonetheless generally take a perspective which focused on the broad interests of the business. In the words of one of the worker directors, 'As far as I am concerned a worker director is there for the betterment of the business. If I see that it is right to have a planned redundancy in the industry in order to achieve the 10 year plan I will let it be known and I don't care if I make enemies – after all the trade unions also agree that there must be a reduction in manpower if the industry is to survive.' (Bank and Jones, 1977, p. 58). The view expressed is very much a directorial one which takes a wide view of the needs of the industry, couched in efficiency terms. It is very clearly not a view from below. The conclusion drawn is that 'There is a logic of institutions and a logic of markets which it is difficult for a worker director to resist. . . . It is for this reason that despite changes in the institutional structure of the BSC scheme to strengthen worker director links with the unions the voices of the worker directors nine years into the scheme sound little different from those heard in the early days.' (Brannen, 1983).

The Post Office Experiment

The above account of the BSC scheme deals with worker directors on divisional boards; such directors were introduced on the corporation's main board in 1978 but no data are extant on the experience. The experiment with worker directors on the main board of the Post Office, launched in the same year, was however the subject of research (Batstone et al., 1983). The Post Office scheme provided for union representatives to sit on the main board and also on regional boards and area policy committees. It was initially set up for a two year period. The main board experiment was terminated at the end of this period, but the experiments at lower levels in the system continued. By the time a decision had to be made as to whether to continue the main board experiment there had been a change of Government. The new administration was not in favour of boardroom participation but adopted a publicly neutral position, leaving it to management and unions to decide. The scheme could only continue if both sides were agreed that it should, but management opposed its continuation and it therefore came to an end (ibid.).

The initial stimulus to set up some system of boardroom participation in the Post Office came from the Labour government in 1974. Both the main unions in the Post Office had been committed to guild socialist ideas in the 1920s and had maintained a positive interest in the area of industrial democracy, apparent in their joint statement of principles concerning its extension, set out in 1974. This document urges that the policy of employee involvement be explored to its limit and that the unions be given positive control over the generation of policies for the industry. Three main reasons are given; first, concerning industrial citizenship, that those working in an organisation should have the right to exercise effective control over decisions that impinge on them; second, that industrial democracy will unleash the talent and ability of the workforce and thus increase the efficiency of the organisation; and finally, as workers have to accept the results of management decisions, they should play a part in formulating them. Management was opposed to boardroom participation, being in favour of increasing participation in an evolutionary way through the extension of current consultative and negotiating arrangements.* Industrial democracy was thought of as a means towards various managerial objectives; the management approach, in contrast to that of the unions, was pragmatic rather than principled. Where industrial democracy was seen as a threat to efficiency, as in boardroom participation, it was not supported (ibid).

Under political pressure the management conceded that there might be a minority of trade union representatives on the board; they would have to be leaders in their unions so that they could contribute special expertise to the board's deliberations. They would also have to accept corporate responsibility and not act in a representational manner. The unions meanwhile proposed a two tier board structure with parity union representation on the supervisory board. The eventual scheme that was elaborated for the main board used a $2X + Y$ formula with a unitary board composed of equal numbers of union and management members and a third independent element jointly agreed between them. The unions were free to appoint their own nominees from within their membership but it was emphasised that they should be high calibre senior union members. On appointment they would have to relinquish negotiating posts and whilst they could not be mandated by their members they could report back to their constituencies.

---

*Until 1970 the Post Office was part of the Civil Service and not a separate corporation. It had elaborate consultative machinery at national, regional and local level derived from the Whitley system in which, from its early days, the post office unions had been deeply involved. (See for example Parris, 1973).

As in the BSC scheme the new worker directors received little guidance on their role; 'in part this was a natural consequence of the general uncertainty over what the experiment involved. They were aware that they were expected to express worker and union interests, to provide a (possibly limited) channel of communication between the board and unions, and to contribute worker knowledge to decisions. At the same time they were aware of their responsibilities as board members for the Post Office.' (ibid). The role of the board itself was also problematic; apart from the more general factors affecting its role which we have discussed earlier in this chapter the Post Office was composed of a number of separate businesses in the postal and telecommunication areas which were run as separately managed entities. In addition the role of the government in relation to the activities of the Post Office actively limited the role of the board. Further, many managers and board members indicated that as a result of the industrial democracy experiment there was a further reduction in the role of the board, a variety of issues being kept from it and determined by other means. Accordingly the board tended to function as a source of legitimation and to an extent a decision-taker, but rarely as a decision-maker (ibid.).

As in the Steel Corporation, worker directors developed over the course of the experiment a network of management contacts; they saw these in part as providing the opportunity for developing alternative analysis of issues, which could be floated in a variety of ways at the board. Management contacts also helped union nominees to understand the patterns of management politics and the way in which they impinged upon views about policy. But these contacts also offered possibilities of mutual influence. Managers might be assured of support of a general kind or over specific issues both at the board and possibly within the unions. Union nominees might be able to influence policy at a formative stage or obtain information to counteract the thrust of papers coming to the board (ibid.).

In contrast to the British Steel case, the union nominees had a formal and effective system of reporting back to union executive committees. They also had discussion sessions with senior union officials. The interest of the unions in boardroom matters, however, tended to be restricted to matters of fairly direct relevance to the routine tasks of the union. In a few cases key union officials believed that the subjects of board debate indicated its limited relevance in general and its near total irrelevance to the unions in particular (ibid.). Whilst in most Post Office unions there were times when the reports of the union nominees played an important role in influencing demands and tactics in negotiations, and formally the unions saw participation at board level as a means of promoting worker interests and influencing the formulation of policy, their traditional forms of organisation and modes of thought — themselves a product of past and present relationships with the Post Office — did not easily permit the unions to pursue this aspiration in practice.

The contributions of the worker directors on the board, as in BSC, tended to be more directly focused on industrial relations and other matters of worker and union interest than those of other board members. Batstone and his colleagues note that there was a further number of factors which limited their contributions. Among these were their acceptance of much of the general management strategy, the nature of their skills, the norm (not always observed) of avoiding negotiation on the board, and the need to accommodate both to the views of other members and to the structuring style of board discussion (ibid.). Nevertheless, union nominees did sway the board on a number of occasions. In some instances they had a considerable impact upon industrial relations issues, in others they provided important inputs into decisions from their knowledge of the Post Office and its staff.

Management members of the board felt that union nominees pursued sectional interests and hence did not share a unity of purpose with other board members; and that they lacked the business skills and knowledge necessary for board debate. These points, together with the excessive size of the board, were seen to discourage discussion by other board members. Management in general in the Post Office felt that they could not identify any significant impact which union nominees had made on the business other than a greater formal emphasis on the manpower implications of policy and some delays in adopting what they saw as the proper course of action. Some argued that managerial freedom had been constrained. Others were not surprised by what they saw as the marginal influence of the union nominees and explained it partly in terms of the calibre of the individuals concerned and partly in terms of the limited role of the board. In the area of industrial relations some managers thought that union nominees had complicated the management task.

The scheme in the Post Office was clearly a structurally more powerful one than that in BSC. It followed the Bullock $2X + Y$ formula in giving trade unions equal representation with management; moreover, the appointment of worker directors was clearly located from the beginning in the trade union structure and reporting back was assumed to be an integral element of the scheme. However, like the BSC worker directors, the Post Office union nominees had to learn, and adapt to, the norms of board conduct; they were dependent upon managerially-structured information and proposals at the board; and they became embedded in a network of informal management contacts. Whilst in the boardroom 'they sought to manipulate board room norms; to challenge management assumptions; and to exploit their network of management contacts', and thus created conflict in some areas of boardroom activity, 'nevertheless their general impact was not significantly greater than that of most worker directors' (ibid).

Worker directors in the private sector

Towers and his colleagues carried out an investigation of worker director schemes in the private sector. They identified eight worker director schemes which satisfied the definition that 'a worker director scheme could be said to exist where a sub-executive employee was appointed to a board within the organisation'. Seven of these schemes were studied. Two of them had been introduced in the 1940s and were related to employee shareholding. The other five had all been introduced in the first half of the 1970s (Towers et al., 1981). All but one of the organisations were in the manufacturing sector and all but two had under 1,000 employees. In contrast to the two public sector schemes all of these schemes were conceived and established by management. In no case was there any pressure or suggestions for the scheme from the workforce or the trade unions. Towers and his colleagues emphasise that in consequence each of the schemes was based on a unitary managerial ideology and had been instituted in order to strengthen or reassert the mechanisms of management control rather than to redistribute that control. In only two of the schemes had there been any trade union involvement in the implementation and appointment of worker directors. Four more of the companies had trade unions; in two of these the trade unions had insisted upon the separation of collective bargaining from the schemes. In the other two the trade unions accepted management's decision to keep the channels separate.

The authors state that although in no case were the worker directors excluded from the formal information that went to the board, they were at a disadvantage in relation to other directors because they were excluded from the informal day-to-day information flows that take place between executive directors. This decreased the possibility of the worker directors having an influence upon strategic policy decisions taken by the board. However, in contrast to the situation in both the Post Office and the Steel Corporation, there was no evidence that the worker directors in these private companies tried to increase their access to information. They go on to argue that the great majority of worker directors were unable to handle effectively even the limited information which was available and did not see the extent to which information could be used as a strategic good. (ibid.). In most of the schemes there was little reporting back between the worker director and employees in the company. This is explained by the constraints of confidentiality surrounding the board, the absence of developed disclosure networks and the existence of alternative channels for the dissemination of information. In the companies concerned, most of which were relatively small, few workers claimed that they had received any information via the worker directors.

The authors argue that 'perhaps the most fundamental quality of the worker director schemes studied here derived from the fact that all of them were originated and most were implemented solely by management' (p. 391). As a result of this, the authors note, management were unlikely to be antagonistic to the schemes; however, they found that many directors felt that the existence of the schemes had had some positive impact on the work of the board. By contrast the evidence suggested that the schemes were not well regarded by the workforce. In the six companies where there were trade unions they were either indifferent to the schemes or ensured that 'the scheme did not cut across the spheres of action of the trade unions or pose any threat to them' (p. 392). The schemes tended therefore to be by-passed or to have little vigour.

Conclusion

The idea of worker directors which emerged into the arena of public discussion and debate in the 1970's was forcibly rejected by management and by much of the formal union structure, despite the TUC's sponsorship of it. In management's case the hostility of the reaction, although usually couched in arguments about efficiency, that is in relation to its effect on the work needs of the organisation, clearly owes much also to management's interest in the organisation as both a political and a career system (Burns, 1969). The board is at once the embodiment of corporate authority, the apex of a managerial career structure, and a source of management power. The introduction of worker directors to the board may well be seen to pose a threat to all three elements.

In the case of the trade unions and their officials the hostility to the notion of worker directors stems from similar sources. Boardroom participation is seen as compromising the independence of trade unions and thus weakening their oppositional power. In so far as appointments to the board are from the trade union within the firm, the authority of shop stewards over and against that of full time officials is enhanced. As a result the organisational career of full time trade union officials, which depends on wielding authority over shop stewards and collective power over employers, is threatened. As both ordinary workers and shop stewards have little to lose in these terms and perhaps something to gain they tend to be more sympathetic to the idea of worker directors.

Whilst the symbolism of the worker director role is clearly potent, the experience of its practice indicates that it poses little threat to the organisation as working system. The worker director schemes in the private sector have been few in number, and in design and operation might best be described by Pateman's term 'pseudo participation'. The public sector schemes were more clearly set up to provide some form of representation of worker interests and in the Post Office scheme, where there was both union involvement and support as well as parity of numbers with employer board representatives, they succeeded, in limited areas, in pursuing those interests. Even within the Post Office scheme, however, the areas where the worker directors were most active, personnel and industrial relations, were not seen by the rest of the board as crucial. The boardroom, moreover, is often not where decision-making takes place; both external constraints and the activities of internal management interest groups can limit the board's scope for decision. In addition, the full time executive board members can operate to structure the nature of information and decisions coming to the board.

The rationalities of capital (including public capital) and labour are different and often competing. Within the boardroom in a market society the dominance of market over other forms of discourse is already established and constantly reinforced by organisational practice. It is necessary for worker directors to learn the language of economic accounting in order to perform a boardroom role; but the language itself involves limitations in the possible forms of that role. Not to learn the language is to be excluded from the action. Worker directors of necessity enter into worlds already established in terms of both formal roles and processes, of custom and practice, of values and language. The social dynamics of those worlds strongly favour the encapsulation of worker directors within the pre-existing boardroom ethos and organisation, and within, though in a limited way, the pre-existing organisational categories of information and analysis.

The paradox of boardroom participation is that if worker representatives are strong enough and willing to put forward competing rationalities they are likely to create conflict in the boardroom, and ensure that the real centres of decision-making move elsewhere, thus rendering themselves impotent in the director role; but if they adopt the director role then their *raison d'être,* from the perspective of the workforce, disappears. This is not to suggest that worker directors do not have effects within organisations which may be seen as beneficial by some groups of actors; nor that the way the scheme is structured is unrelated to its impact. What the evidence does seem to indicate is that this form of worker participation does not seem to transform or undermine management authority in any significant way.

Further Reading

Brookes (1979) usefully summarises much of the theoretical and empirical material on the role of the board within industry. Gustavsen (1976) is also relevant. The Bullock Report is a key document in the British context; Elliot (1978) and Clark et al. (1980) provide background to the debate about Bullock. Reports of management, trade union and worker attitudes toward Bullock and of high level participation can be found in Knight (1979), Dowling et al. (1981) and Cressey et al. (1981). Marsden (1978) offers a comparison of the Bullock Report with the Sudreau Report in France and the Biedenkopf Report in Germany in the context of the industrial relations culture of each country and the methods of industrial relations regulation. Batstone and Davies (1976) provide a short summary of European experience with worker director schemes; in this context see also Brannen et al. (1976), Chapter Eleven. Kuhne (1980) provides a review of the issues raised by worker director schemes for the management of multinational companies and some interesting data on the approach of American multinational management towards such schemes. Case studies of worker director schemes can be found in Emery and Thorseud (1969), Batstone et al. (1983), Chell (1980) and Brannen et al. (1976). Bank and Jones (1977) provide the published response of the BSC worker directors to the academic study of the experiment in which they were involved. Brannen (1983) is, in part, a reply.

7 · Participation and Political Economy

A number of economic thinkers have seen workers' participation as anti-pathetic to efficiency, arguing that it distorts decision-making and has a negative economic impact on investment, wage levels, the expansion and contraction of employment and so on. This applies even if the form of participation does not weaken management's ultimate authority, but does alter the way that authority can be exercised through the decision-making process. There is, however, no body of work of a theoretical or substantive kind within economic thinking on workers' participation as such. As Hunter has commented, 'From a strictly economic point of view, once we depart from a pure profit-maximising assumption on the one hand or a worker self-management model on the other we find ourselves in no man's land.' (Hunter, 1980, p. 44.) The points advanced tend to be derived from the thinking of labour economists about the collective bargaining process or 'are more often than not statements of belief, sometimes based on "experiences of industrial life" and sometimes on rather vague evidence from other countries'. (p. 35).

The arguments tend to be of the following kind. Employers and workers (trade unions) will have different preferences. The outcome of increased participation will be to move decisions away from employers' preferences towards trade unions' preferences. For example, in an expanding industry the management of companies will prefer to expand as much as possible; whereas unions will prefer to increase wages so that the amount of expansion which takes place will be less than that which is possible. In a contracting industry the management will prefer to reduce wages and unions will resist this; they will also resist redundancies. Participation therefore leads to higher wages and less employment, higher prices and some substitution of imported for home-produced goods, thus fuelling the inflationary spiral. The trade unions will also resist investment in new machinery and thus hold back the economic development of the firm. Moreover the introduction of participation will lead to a reduction in 'business confidence' and the supply of capital to firms will dry up (Clifton, 1978; Hunter, 1980).

The employer representatives on the Bullock Committee argued against worker representation on the board because 'it might provoke the confrontation or extend the scope of collective bargaining into top level decision-making' (Bullock, 1977). The reaction of industrial interests to the

Bullock proposals was also to stress that worker directors on the board would 'do harm to business performance by demotivating management, slowing down managerial decision-making, and driving foreign investment out of the country' (Elliot, 1978, p. 242). Worker directors, then, would move collective bargaining to a higher level and extend its range into topics hitherto subject to managerial control. Similar arguments are used against other forms of worker participation which allow a degree of control over managerial decision-making.

A number of points can be made about these arguments. In relation to investment starvation, only 10-15% of investment funds are raised on the open market (Hunter, 1980.) Other than in the short term the market tends to react to performance rather than to aspects of the internal organisation of the firm. More generally, many of these arguments assume (and this is common to most economic thinking) that management will behave in an economically rational way in its decision-making and that workers will place self-interest before the general interest of the firm or the wider community. We have seen in early chapters the complexity of factors that affect management and worker orientations. In that context the assumptions behind this form of economic analysis might be seen to be ideological rather than logial, and somewhat simple-minded. Moreover, in relation to collective bargaining on wages there is considerable disagreement between economists about the existence of a 'mark up': that is the supposed difference between the market wage and a wage achieved through collective bargaining (Metcalf. 1977). One author has recently argued that in both Britain and the USA 'unions have had a negligible impact on the money wage level and therefore that market forces have determined the rate of wage inflation' (Mulvey, 1978). In addition there are considerable difficulties in generalising from issues surrounding wage bargaining (where objectives are relatively short term, the information available to unions limited and seen as partial because it is presented by management as part of their bargaining strategy, and relationships traditionally adversarial) to the different context of workers or trade union representatives participating in some aspects of the decision-making process. It is also the case that whilst unions tend to resist rendundancies, the most massive shedding of labour in the post-war period has taken place in industries that were highly unionised, and have strong collective bargaining, and other forms of worker participation. Coal, steel, and shipbuilding might serve as examples. Recent evidence also suggests that in relation to technical change as much, if not more resistance, is to be found in the boardroom, as on the shop floor (Northcott, 1980). Finally, as we saw in an earlier chapter, there is little evidence that worker directors act in ways different from other board members in British industry or materially affect the decision-making process of the firm.

Many of the economic arguments against worker participation appear to mirror Weber. In the first chapter we saw how Weber argued that the appropriation of job rights by workers or the existence of rights to participate in management were inimical to formal economic rationality, that is a calculative approach to economic ends. Formal rationality, it needs to be noted, is not the same thing as efficiency and Weber did not equate the two (Albrow, 1970, pp. 63-6). Efficiency can be defined as the attainment of a particular goal with the least possible detriment to other goals and is commonly measured through the calculation of costs in terms of money, time, or energy (ibid.). The achievement of efficiency needs to take account of issues of substantive rationality. In this chapter we examine some of the evidence on the relationships between worker participation and economic efficiency, looking at the work group, the firm and society as a whole. At the level of the work group the focus is on work attitudes and job satisfaction, at that of the firm on decision-making processes, and at the level of society on social integration, both historically and currently.

Participation, productivity and the work group

Blumberg, in reviewing the literature on experiments on participation, has concluded that despite the diversity of the literature and research and of the characteristics of the population studied there is an amazing consistency in the findings. 'There is hardly a study in the entire literature which fails to demonstrate that satisfaction in work is enhanced or that other generally acknowledged beneficial consequences accrue from a genuine increase in workers' decision-making power.' (Blumberg, 1968, p. 123). It needs to be noted however that most of Blumberg's evidence is related to participation at the level of the work group.

In an analysis of the early Hawthorn experiments and of writing based on them, Blumberg argues that if one seeks to explain the improvements resulting from the famous Test room experiments concretely (a remarkable increase in productivity and an equally impressive decline in work alienation) one can point to three possible social changes which might have been responsible: first, the transformation of traditional patterns of industrial power or authority which allowed the workers to determine the conditions of their work; second, the creation among the workers of a cohesive primary group; third, the enhanced status the workers gained from participating in the experiment (the Hawthorne effect). He argues that whilst most accounts tend to emphasise the social and status effects there is little reference to issues of industrial power and control. In so far as enhanced status was a factor in the workers' improved efficiency and satisfaction, 'then one must recognise that it was the increased power of the workers which enhanced their status' (p. 43)*.

*There are alternative explanations. Carey, for example, in a re-examination of the data from the Hawthorne studies, has argued that increases in production can be explained as a result of close supervision and discipline (Carey, 1967). This is in contradiction to Blumberg's analysis which argued the 'almost total disappearance of externally imposed discipline and supervision' (Blumberg, 1968, p. 34). For a critique from within psychology of the job satisfaction literature see also Wall and Lischeron, 1977.

Blumberg claims that this analysis, concentrating on industrial authority at the workgroup level, finds support in other studies (although because of the way in which the human relations and neo-human relations movements developed, it does not always deal adequately with issues of power and authority). A study conducted in the mid-1940s by Coch and French at the Harwood Company, a clothing manufacturing firm, is used as an example. The plant employed 600 workers, mostly long-serving and mostly female. The experiments were set up in the context of management attempts to change production methods and of worker resistance to this. Four groups of workers were selected and similar job changes introduced for each group. One group had the job changes imposed on it. The second discussed them with management through their representatives and the other two were total participation groups where all members of the group were involved in the decisions about job re-design. The non-participatory groups showed a high degree of hostility to the change; 17% of the group left the firm within 40 days, there were marked expressions of aggression against management, a high level of grievance behaviour, and productivity fell markedly from the pre-change level. The indirect participation group lost no members, there was co-operation with management in introducing the change and after a short learning period, production levels exceeded those before the change. The total participation groups were the most successful; within two days of the change they had achieved their pre-change level of production and they went on to exceed it by some 14% (Coch and French, 1948). Blumberg concludes that 'stated in the most general terms, the researchers found that "success" in bringing about job changes – defined both in terms of productivity and worker satisfaction – was directly proportional to the amount of worker participation.' (Blumberg, 1968, p. 83).

By the 1960s it was possible for Tannebaum and his colleagues to argue, on the basis of two decades of research, that worker participation at the level of the work group was likely to lead to a higher rate of output, better quality work, reduction in labour turnover and grievance behaviour, greater readiness to accept change and an improvement in the quality of management decisions. (Tannebaum et al., 1961). It was clear also by this time that the relationships between work group participation and efficiency were not simple. The same study notes that efficiency outcomes are dependent on a number of conditional factors, including the ability of the work group to be involved in the relevant activities, their support for the outcome, and the absence of any threat to the job security of the workers. Blumberg is also aware that enhanced control within the work group is not sufficient in itself. He notes that after the first few years of the Hawthorne experiments productivity ceased to rise and in the final stages of the study fell. 'Threatened unemployment, especially towards the final days of the study, undoubtedly had an adverse effect upon productivity and morale.' (Blumberg, 1968, p. 40). Other factors however also need to be considered.

French and his colleagues attempted to repeat the Harwood experiments in a Norwegian shoe factory employing 1600 workers. Nine groups were involved in the experiment, five as experimental groups and four as control groups. Work groups in this factory already set their own production rates according to a piece-work system. The experimental groups had their decision-making power expanded to encompass work assignment between work groups, levels of training, and division of labour within the work group. The experimental groups showed no improvement in productivity over the control groups, though they returned to the pre-change level of output more quickly than the control groups; they also displayed slightly more work satisfaction (French et al., 1960). The Norwegian factory was unionised and the workers there were accustomed to negotiate change through their union representatives; the experiment cut across this norm; the work groups also, on the basis of previous experience, felt that increases in production were likely to cut piece rates so they resisted change in the production norm. Finally, the items that they were allowed to decide on were of less importance than items over which they already had control, particularly the level of production. We can note that the Norwegian workers already had a set of democratic values related to work organisation.

By the early 1960s Norway had reached a stage where, according to one commentator, continued increases in productivity could no longer be achieved through conventional methods such as scientific management or an exclusive reliance on technological development. Instead it was seen as necessary to seek new ways of utilising the human resources available in working life, through changes in the organisation of work. From the middle 1960s a series of work group participation experiments was launched. A leading proponent of these experiments argued in a recent book evaluating them that 'Blumberg's well-known point that there is hardly an investigation which does not show that work satisfaction increases after an increase in the decision-making rights of the workers generally applies to the Norwegian developments. Measurements were not always made, nor are those made always comparable. But as an overall impression this clearly holds.' (Gustavsen and Hunnius, 1981, p. 68). In relation to productivity, again no unequivocal picture emerges in relation to Norway but 'it seems fairly clear that improvements in productivity occurred in most cases, provided that productivity is given a broad definition' (p. 68). Included in such a broad definition is the ability of workforces to be flexible and adaptable in relation to a changing market and product environment. It is worth noting that 'the productivity argument accounts for much of the management interest that emerged in relation to the industrial democracy programme' (p. 70); but also, in Norway, the trade union movement in the post-war period was in favour of a movement towards high productivity. 'The relatively strong position of the trade unions, their link to the governing Labour party, and a strong faith in state socialism probably explains why the union movement found it possible to back productivity in the belief that this would be best for society as a whole.' (ibid.).

A similar series of experiments was carried out in Sweden at about the same time. In the words of the technical director of the Swedish Employers' Association in 1973, 'The goal is to find work forms which result in increased productivity, better job satisfaction and a better environment. The impulse behind the experiments has been industry's growing difficulty in recruiting and keeping production personnel.' (Lindholme, 1978). In Sweden as in Norway there was a joint union-management approach to these issues. In the course of the 1970s the trade unions became sceptical about this form of participation. In particular they realised that it was dependent on and made little alteration to managerial prerogative; and it did not alter the distribution of power and authority. This led to the trade union movement moving its support away from a consensual approach to one based on work reform (Brannen and Caswill, 1978). A related point has been made by Kelly, who on the basis of an analysis of 200 cases of work re-organisation notes that whilst workers may increase control over their work tasks this does not necessarily mean an elimination of managerial control, and that such changes often lead to a simultaneous increase in overall managerial control of performance (Kelly, 1980, p. 29).

The experiments that have been described do seem to have achieved increases in productivity and economic efficiency; they allowed and facilitated technical change and they had some impact on issues of recruitment, manning and absenteeism. They achieved this through increasing the influence and control workers had over their immediate work environment. It is important to note, however, that the literature does not deal with the effect of these changes over time. Moreover, as Daniel points out, much of the literature on this form of participation has tended to focus on workplaces where a unitary view of the enterprise prevailed, the workforce was non-unionised and located in a semi-rural environment 'with none of the history of mass unemployment, prolonged and bitter battles with employers for union recognition and minimum rights which tend to characterise industrial areas' (Daniel, 1973, p. 57). In the Scandinavian cases, although the experiments were undertaken in a unionised context it was one of apparent consensus between management, unions and workforce. In addition, within both Norway and Sweden, whilst the unions are powerful at a national level they have little bargaining strength at the level of the plant.

Most of these approaches have focused on what Daniel has termed the 'work context', that is, on the attitudes, motivations and satisfactions of workers, their relationships to technology through the work group, and the quality of inter-personal contact between them and the work group. The same process is seen as producing psychological and social benefits for the workforce and economic benefits for employers. However, as Kelly has pointed out, workers' needs and interests in job design are not confined to psychological aspects such as self-actualisation or job satisfaction; 'they also extend into economic issues such as labour intensity, job security and wage levels, as one indeed would predict from a knowledge of the fundamentally economic character of the employment relationship' (Kelly, 1980, p. 31). Missing from the descriptions of the experiments seems to be any discussion of the distribution of economic rewards from the changes in work organisation. Daniel has termed this the 'bargaining context'; he argues that implicit in this context is the notion that 'work and change represent disutility for the worker, and consequently taking on more work and accepting change has to be compensated for' (Daniel, 1973, p. 58.).

Participation, productivity and bargaining

Participation in changes to work organisation in the United Kingdom has to a great extent taken place in the 'bargaining context', as one would expect in an economy with a strong shop steward movement at workplace level. One form of this has been productivity bargaining. The early productivity bargains involved negotiations about management proposals for changes in work practice. Even in the original Fawley case, however, the management proposals arose out of extensive discussions in the refinery in which shop stewards played a major part (Flanders, 1964). The core of productivity bargaining was agreement over changes in the wage-effort ratio. The deals struck all centred around controlling overtime, reducing manning, and creating greater flexibility of task arrangements within sectors of the workforce. The exchange took the form of increased earnings for the workforce and lower costs and increased productivity for management. Of the early productivity bargains Clegg has written that they achieved 'substantial reductions in the unit costs' (Clegg, 1980, p. 145). Regarding later bargains there is dispute over the extent of the economic effects.

In once sense productivity bargaining removed and was designed to remove shop floor controls over various types of work practices. In another, it opened up possibilities for extending control by challenging traditional modes of behaviour amongst both management and unions. Productivity bargaining required new ways of thinking and made new demands on managers and supervisors. It encouraged and formalised planning and enhanced the role of personnel and industrial relations managements (McKersie and Hunter, 1973). It also increased the degree of workers' participation. 'It recognises that major industrial relations decisions are taken at plant level and strengthens and enhances the quality of industrial relations by increasing the frequency and range of plant consultation. Moreover workers and work groups are much more directly involved in decisions, thus strengthening industrial democracy. Furthermore such changes normally mean that workers are given an opportunity to exercise abilities more fully, which in turn leads to an increase in job satisfaction. Finally it highlights deficiencies in trade union organisation and expertise and encourages them to repair deficiencies in staff and supporting services.' (Cotgrove et al., 1971).

Cotgrove and his colleagues explored one of the later generation of productivity bargains in which both the 'work context' and the 'bargaining context' were taken into account. A general agreement was reached between the company and the unions for more efficient manpower utilisation together with changes in pay and conditions. At plant level there was extensive participation by the workforce in the reorganisation of work. The changes which resulted comprised the setting up of a joint management/union works council, and a structure of shift meetings and foremen's discussion groups below this. Any issues could be discussed within these structures but also taken out from them and passed into the normal negotiating machinery. At the level of work organisation operatives planned and organised their own work and there was job enlargement, combining previously separated tasks into one job. The payment system was also changed from the previous fixed manual salary.

These changes resulted in a 20% increase in output from a labour force that was 20% smaller than before the changes took place. Labour turnover reduced but absenteeism increased (in part this was explained by an improvement in sickness benefits). Although the authors argue that it is difficult to separate the effect of technological changes in increasing efficiency from that of changes in satisfaction on operators' performance, 'it is problematic whether certain of these technical changes would have been accepted by the operatives outside of this general context of change' (p. 126). The initial attraction of the scheme to the workforce was the promise of higher earnings in relation to work load. 'Subsequently however, after implementation, the changes were regarded favourably more because of the way the changes in working practice increased intrinsic rewards rather than because of the increases in earnings.' (Daniel, 1973, p. 58).

Flanders claimed that productivity bargaining allowed unions to share power with management (Flanders, 1970). In a recent assessment of the long run effects of productivity bargaining Gallie suggests that it neither had this effect nor that of decreasing worker control and shifting power decisively back to management (Gallie, 1978). He argues that shop steward power in the refineries he studied derived 'above all from their ability to represent the workforce in the crucial negotiations between full time officials and management over changes in work organisation, and in this...productivity bargaining heightened rather than diminished their status in the workforce' (p. 172). It both increased the stewards' role vis-à-vis full-time officials and brought them into more frequent contact with the upper echelons of management and the longer range organisation problems of the refineries. In addition productivity bargaining led to the recognition that questions of work organisation had to be negotiated and agreed and it formalised the right of control; it forced management to put forward its longer term objectives and provided better institutional machinery for vetting management proposals. 'Productivity bargaining consolidated and made more effective powers of control that the representatives already had acquired and it extended their formal control to the entire sphere of work organisation.' (p. 174). On the other hand, management power was in no profound sense challenged. Management still initiated change, and had superior organisational means for assessing its design and implications, and for costing it. The type of power productivity bargaining gave to stewards was essentially negative: 'the discussions remained then discussions between unequals and although productivity bargaining strengthened steward power it can hardly be said to have led to the sharing of that power.' (p. 176).

Equality, participation and economy

In an extension of the productivity bargaining model McCarthy and Ellis suggested that unions and management should increasingly engage in 'predicative bargaining', that is bargaining around the broad corporate strategy of the firm (McCarthy and Ellis, 1973). Here, there would no longer be any room for a doctrine of employer-reserved rights or managerial prerogative. The need for it, they argued, derived from the increasing power of trade unions within the workplace — 'the power from within' — and the changing nature of power 'from without', that is, the demands of the rapidly changing political, cultural, economic and technical environment. The answer was to increase participation through a system of joint decision-making which they termed 'management by agreement'. What they propose is not a system of workers' control 'but it is the most meaningful way of promoting the aims of workers' participation in management and the ideas of industrial democracy . . . it does not seek to slur over or disregard the ultimate responsibilities of management for the overall conduct of the enterprise' (p. 186). Management by agreement, that is participative forms of management, is essential for companies 'if a business is to grow and prosper or even survive'. In the case of the government and the community at large, 'success in this area may truly be said to hold the key to progress in other important fields — not least the restoration of Britain's competitive edge' (p. 199).

The view set out by McCarthy and Ellis is essentially normative. Some of the mechanisms of the process have been set out by Gallie: 'in cultures in which the value of equality has salience, the less participative the decision-making system — in the sense of the effective capacity of both workers and their representatives to influence the formal institutional machinery — the greater will be the tension in management/worker relations, and the more likely it is that the firm will be viewed as exploitative.' (p. 207). Gallie's general proposition is based on a number of sub-propositions. The less participative the decision-making system the less legitimate it will appear. Lower legitimacy will be associated with higher degrees of distrust of management. This will mean that management decisions will be unacceptable and that conditions will not be conducive to the acceptance of change. Management will have to use external constraints to impose its decisions and hostility to management will be reinforced. The system of work organisation will not be well adapted to the needs and expectations of the workforce. Dissatisfaction with the system of work organisation will in turn contribute to an unfavourable image of management. There will be a generalised sense of insecurity leading to anxiety, which will find expression in an increased suspicion of management's intentions and, again, a higher level of hostility to management. When conflict occurs it will be intense. 'A low participative system, then, by enhancing normative conflict, by increasing the likelihood that major decisions will be experienced as coercive, by reducing satisfactions derived from the work environment, by creating a generalised sense of insecurity, and by enhancing the intensity of overt conflict, will tend to generate an alienative attitude to the firm. Management will be viewed with distrust and be regarded as exploitative.' (p. 210).

Within society and between sectors of the economy the values placed on equality and on participation are likely to be different. We have in earlier chapters discussed some factors that will affect this. Between societies these values are also likely to vary. Goldthorpe has put forward the proposition that 'secular changes in the form of stratification evident in British society may be taken as the most developed manifestation of tendencies or potentialities which are in fact generally present in the societies of the advanced capitalist world'* (Goldthorpe: 1978 p. 197). He argues that over recent decades the general rise in the rate of inflation reflects a situation in which conflict between social groups and strata has become more intense and more equally matched, in a process of mutual reinforcement. In the case of Britain he identifies three interrelated aspects of such a situation: the decay of the status order, the realisation of citizenship, and the emergence of a mature working class.

By the first he means a process whereby the status order (that is the set of beliefs about the criteria of social worth or superiority) is progressively weakened and disrupted by various forces that are in fact associated with the functioning of an advanced economy; processes of urbanisation, geographical mobility and the extension of the market principle of equal exchange lead to uncertainty and dissension as to how status is to be attributed. 'More seriously, the very notion of generalised social worth and superiority which are crucial to the status order are called into question and tend to break down; and thus as socially constructed reality, the phenomenon of prestige itself decomposes.' (p. 199). Once the normative ordering of status is removed there is no reason, he argues, why subordinate groups should not raise new challenges 'both via their organisations and directly, to the authority of employers and managements — or, to be more accurate, to the power which the latter have in the past derived from the status order over and above their authority as functionally and legally grounded.' (p. 200).

*Other writers have argued that there are features of the British situation that make it a special case — see Gilbert, 1981. A critique of the general argument put forward by Goldthorpe can be found in Smith, 1982.

'Realisation of citizenship' refers to Marshall's argument, discussed in earlier chapters, that the working through of the principles of citizenship in recent times is towards extending rights in the sphere of production. Goldthorpe instances pressure for rights in jobs and rights to work, and the concern of unions to be involved as of right 'in all decision-making processes which affect their members' employment conditions and prospects.' (p. 203). Whilst the decay of the status order has freed workers from inhibiting notions of their own inferiority, and the growth of citizenship has meant the widening and strengthening of forms of political and industrial action open to them, the full impact of these changes will only be experienced 'as a working class develops whose members have grown up entirely under the new conditions that have been created' (p. 205).

Britain, he argues, has a more 'mature' working class than other industrial nations, in the demographic sense that the vast majority of the industrial workforce were already settled urban dwellers by the early part of the twentieth century. This urbanised workforce is only marginally diluted by recruitment from non-industrial populations such as rural workers, and is largely self-recruiting. 'Maturity' has also a socio-political sense. In Britain the working class has not only been in the vanguard of the struggle for citizenship rights but has been able to develop them without the discontinuity which arises from dictatorship, civil war, or occupation. Such a mature working class will have a strong commitment to these rights and the organisations that underpin them, and will have the potential for concerted economic or political action.

Goldthorpe's argument, then, is that there has been a number of changes of both a structural and cultural kind within British society which have produced a working class that is both willing and able to 'punch its weight'. Inflation, within this framework, has been an expression of distributional conflict, with a working class ready and able to engage forcefully in it. Behind the economic problem of inflation lies the threat 'that the social divisions and antagonisms arising from an increasingly delegitimated structure of class inequality will prove no longer capable of institutional containment' (p. 208).

Elsewhere, as we saw in Chapter Three, Goldthorpe has argued that if worker power is not to be used in a purely defensive or negative way there must be an end to inequality, one element of which is inequality of access to control over industrial decision-making processes (Goldthorpe, 1974). Similarly, Fox remarks that 'the galloping contagion of distrust is well represented in the concept of galloping inflation' (Fox, 1974, p. 322). Whilst he is sceptical about the possibility of a total reversal of the tendencies in industrial market society leading to distrust, he urges the need to improve trust relations, if we can, to bring under control our more chronic problems of inflation and economic stagnation (p. 356). One element in such a strategy of improvement would be the need to re-examine 'the numerous conventions governing decision-making and rewards in work organisations for their relevance and fairness' (p. 358). Crouch too states that 'where there is no trust there can be no cooperation and everything must be governed by one-sided domination or very short term bargaining. In such situations there will be extreme reluctance to forgo current consumption and any attempt by one side to erect an ostensibly neutral constraint will be suspected of bias.' (Crouch, 1978, p. 233). He goes on to suggest that the more workers' representatives are involved in the control of economic variables the less likely they will be to pursue their own short term interests, and notes (in Durkheimian vein) that the three societies (Sweden, West Germany and Japan) that have been particularly successful in combining high growth, full employment and low rates of inflation also evinced 'advanced, though highly varied, forms of integration of organised social interests' (p. 230).

Conclusion

There is relatively clear evidence that various forms of participation at the level of the work organisation, to bring about task changes, can and have had positive economic effects for the organisation concerned. The conditions for success will however vary from organisation to organisation depending on the already existing level of participation of the workforce in each case and the degree of institutionalisation of labour relations in the wider economy. Where there is already a high degree of institutionalisation changes in work organisation can only be achieved by means of participatory channels in the wider decision-making structure of the firm. Productivity bargaining exemplifies this. We have also seen that worker participation in work organisation does not necessarily pose any challenge to the authority of management in the workplace. Nevertheless, this is not to argue that the effects are trivial, as Ramsay suggests (Ramsay, 1977). It is possible to increase worker power and in certain respects diminish that of management without eroding managerial authority. The frontier of participation is made up of many elements.

The relationship between worker participation and the operation of the economy, either at the level of the firm or at the level of the society, are complex. A formal view of market rationality, and one that is widely articulated, suggests that worker participation operates against the interests of economic effectiveness. The nature of the material presented in this chapter suggests that such a view rests on assumptions of dubious validity about the nature of industrial society and its social system, and on a restrictive and short term view of economy. This is not to argue that economic efficiency can only be achieved through the use of participation. Whilst, for example, the introduction of worker participation in Chile under the Allende Government was associated with improvements in economic performance (Espinosa and Zimbalist, 1978) it improved even more under the economic and political autocracy of General Pinochet, as one recent commentator has pointed out (De Bylder, 1981).

Within advanced political and industrial structures, however, the evidence strongly suggests that long term economic efficiency and stability cannot be achieved without a substantial measure of worker participation. Certainly, underlying the arguments of writers like Goldthorpe there is the notion of a working class which, through its increasing cultural and institutional maturity, has the power to destabilise and render inefficient the current market economy system. We have seen in earlier chapters the way in which interest in participation has historically ebbed and flowed in relation to the market power of labour, and we shall return to that point in the concluding chapter. In Goldthorpe's analysis, on the other hand, the notion is implicit that there can be no major reversal of the trend. Starting from a different perpsective a similar view has been taken by the economic commentator Peter Jay (Jay, 1977a). For him, classic capitalism is no longer viable because there is no longer any possibility of restoring a market based on bargaining between individual agents. Since he rejects the idea of totalitarian government as the co-ordinator of the factors of production, and capital can no longer freely perform this role, he suggests that 'a general system of workers' co-operatives in a market economy offers the only chance of reconciling high employment with currency stability and democratic government, because it is the only way that collective bargaining can be put to sleep' (Jay, 1977b). This however raises questions about the relationship of economic democracy to worker participation, and it is to some of these that we turn in the next chapter.

Further Reading

Vanek (1975) provides some theoretical material; the lack of development of economic thinking in this area is indicated by the fact that although the main criterion for selection into the volume was that the articles should be economic, most of the material presented consists of political and institutional analysis. Heathfield (1977) provides a more focused volume of economic analysis of both German and British experience. See also I.E.A. (1977) and Hunter (1980). Berg et al. (1978) and Wall and Lischeron (1977) offer critical accounts of the effects of experiments in work organisation and stand as a useful counterweight to Blumberg (1968). See also Kelly (1982). Case studies of productivity bargaining can be found in Flanders (1964) and Cotgrove et al. (1971). McKersie and Hunter (1973) provide a general account of the experiences of productivity bargaining and Gallie (1978) sets out a recent assessment of its effects on management and shop steward control. Fox (1974a), Goldthorpe (1978), Crouch (1978), and critical assessments of Goldthorpe in Gilbert (1981) and Smith (1982) place the issue of worker participation in the broader contexts of social stratification and macroeconomic policy.

8 · Economic Democracy

In previous chapters we have largely been concerned with participation and industrial democracy where capital, either private or state, owned the means of production. Here we look at the implications for worker participation of workers becoming involved in ownership, either directly through investing or indirectly through the social ownership of industry. The main focus of interest is on whether worker ownership affects the involvement of the worker in the enterprise, the nature of relationships between workers and managers, and in particular the relationships of authority and coordination. Initially we look at a form of sub-economic democracy, the financial participation of employees within the capitalist enterprise.

Sub-economic democracy

We have seen in Chapter Two how financial participation schemes of various kinds have been in operation in Britain since the second half of the nineteenth century. Although there had been occasional and informal profit sharing schemes earlier it was only with a change in company law in 1865 that the payment of bonuses and the acquisition of shares could be put on a regular basis. The motivations and aims of nineteenth century employers introducing profit sharing ranged from the philanthropy of Quaker employers like Seebohm Rowntree to cynical attempts to dislodge trade unions or prevent their spread (Bristow, 1974).

The motives of employers who introduced such schemes have been categorized as relating to goals of equality, incentive, participation, and deterrence (Creigh et al., 1981). The argument from equality for financial participation is based on the notion that capital and labour both contribute to the creation of profit and that any surplus accruing after both employees and shareholders have been paid adequately should be divided. The incentive argument for profit sharing is that if an employee is given a share in company profits then she or he will be motivated to work hard and to make those profits as large as possible. The participation argument is related to this, suggesting that profit sharing attaches workers to the firm and creates a co-operative spirit in the enterprise which will facilitate the achievement of enterprise goals. Finally, the deterrence argument is that financial participation will deter employees from engaging in individual or collective action against the firm. Clearly a number of these goals interrelate.

During the course of the nineteenth century and into the first two decades of the twentieth, interest in profit sharing came in fits and starts. In the turbulent period after the first world war there was a growth in profit sharing, and in attempts to make it part of government policy and to legislate to confer tax and other advantages on profit sharing firms. These attempts failed. The Ministry of Reconstruction concluded that better industrial relations should be founded on something other than a cash basis. The trade unions and the Labour party were hostile on the grounds that profit sharing was an employer weapon against the unions. Whilst some large employers such as Sir Alfred Mond and Lord Leverhulme set up profit sharing schemes that have continued in one form or another to the present day, and profit sharing became part of Liberal, and subsequently Conservative party, philosophy, there was no development or renaissance of interest until the 1970s (Bristow, 1974).

Financial participation schemes are of two main kinds; first, those involving a cash distribution to categories of employees, which may be based on a percentage of profits or be otherwise profit-linked, or related to dividends paid on share capital. Cash-based schemes may also be related to performance and productivity and paid as a collective bonus; the Rucker and Scanlon plans, based on some variant of value added, are examples of these. The second main type of financial participation is share-based; shares are distributed to employees as a form of profit bonus. These shares can be either voting or non-voting and are usually the latter. A British Institute of Management report in 1976 found that of the then existing cash-based schemes half had come into existence in the previous five years and that this constituted a significant net increase in the number of schemes existing previously (Lloyd, 1976). Prior to 1977 only ten companies with over 10,000 employees had any schemes of financial participation and Elliot estimates that 'there were in 1977 barely 100 schemes in the UK for employees (though there were 1,000 for top executives)' (Elliot, 1978, p. 185). There has been a marked increase since that time, partly owing to changes in the Finance Act, and partly as a result of political support for the development of such schemes from both the Conservative and Liberal parties. A recent survey covering all sectors of industry suggests that share-based schemes operated in some 14% of establishments, all of them in the private sector. Almost all of these have been introduced since 1970 (Daniel and Millward, 1983).

The trade union movement continues to be wary of share-ownership schemes. In 1974 the TUC argued that such schemes provided no control over managerial decision-making; the issue of shares, for example, did not usually involve voting rights. The annual profit shareout therefore was simply seen by workers in the same way as an annual bonus. There was no advantage and considerable disadvantage to workers in tying up their savings in the firm that employed them. It doubled their insecurity in that both job and savings would be lost if the firm collapsed. The TUC further argued that such schemes do little or nothing to reduce the inequality of wealth (TUC, 1974). The general attitude of the TUC has not however prevented groups of trade unionists and individual unions from accepting such schemes.

Whilst the TUC was antagonistic to profit sharing schemes of the kind just described it did in 1973 express some support for the creation of a national capital sharing scheme based on a national workers' fund. The proposal, which echoed ideas being developed in Denmark, required companies to transfer 1% of their equity shares each year to a national workers' fund. All workers in both public and private sectors would participate in the fund, which would be run by a governing council with a TUC majority. 'The fund would be free to exercise full ownership rights through its shareholdings, including the right to nominate workers to attend shareholders' meetings. It would operate as a sort of workers' unit trust and would, said the report, be governed by rules which emphasised its social role, including safeguarding prospects for employment.' (Elliot, 1978, p. 189). A similar but much more radical plan was put forward by the Swedish manual workers' union ILO; it has become known as the Meidner plan after the name of its main author. The main thrust of the Meidner plan is that private companies should contribute to wage earner investments funds in the form of compulsory direct stock issues. The plan suggests that 20% of profits be transferred each year to wage earner funds. There would be a number of funds on a regional or a trade union basis. The dividends earned on employee-owned capital would be transferred into a central fund. The money from the central fund would be used for the benefit of all wage earners to provide training, research and so on. The idea was that within a relatively short period of time, a few decades, the majority of shares in large companies would be owned by the employee fund. Whilst the Meidner report was accepted by the ILO congress in June 1976 it did not, at that time, gain support within the political system. It remained, however, the subject of discussion and elaboration (Elvander, 1979, p. 159); its implementation in some form was part of the manifesto commitment of the Social Democratic Government elected in the autumn of 1982.

We have noted earlier the various aims that managements may have in introducing financial participation schemes. If the schemes do not affect managerial control of decision-making or the distribution of wealth, then clearly they do not fulfil any equality objective. Whilst there is little evidence about their direct impact as incentives, since the rewards from such schemes do not relate to individual effort or (depending on the type of technology) very much to labour effort at all, they are unlikely to have much effect. They might on the other hand be seen as affecting the worker's general feeling of attachment to the firm and indirectly, by for example reducing industrial conflict, the general efficiency of the organisation.

A recent survey of all sectors of industry suggests that this might be the case. The incidence of industrial action is generally related to size of firm or establishment, with larger units having a higher incidence (Smith, et al., 1978). Controlling for size Daniel and Millward discovered that, in industry in general, establishments with under 100 workers with financial participation schemes had a lower than average incidence of industrial action, but that for establishments with more than 100 employees it was not possible to explore the relationship. They conclude however that 'a connection between widespread share ownership and industrial peace is not entirely fanciful' (Daniel and Millward, 1983). Whilst this data is indicative, it needs to be treated with caution because not all sectors of the workforce are necessarily part of the profit sharing schemes, and the data cannot explore the relationship between membership of schemes and strike action. Gray however, on the basis of a detailed study of one Scanlon plan and a review of literature on others, suggested that they had little impact on industrial disputes or absenteeism. He argues that there is no convincing account of any such scheme being successful (Gray, 1971).

Studies in the USA, where employee financial incentive schemes are more widespread (it is estimated (Metzger, 1981) that some 300,000 firms have profit sharing plans), suggests that the effect on employee attachment and company performance is positive. Conte and Tannenbaum for example, have argued, on the basis of a survey of management in 98 companies, that the existence of employee ownership plans had a substantial positive effect on the attitudes of employees towards the firm and that this was stronger where employees held their shares directly rather than through a trust. The same study indicated that management thought that employee ownership improved productivity and increased profits (Conte and Tannenbaum, 1978). Long has also concluded, on the basis of a study at a small transport company, that employee ownership has a positive effect on organisational identification, job attitudes and organisational performance (Long, 1978); however, 'although share ownership does in and of itself appear to have beneficial effects on certain job attitudes, employee participation in decision-making appears to have stronger effects' (p. 762). Since it cannot be assumed that employee share ownership will automatically lead to this increased participation, conscious efforts to increase employee participation must be made. He adds however that employee ownership may create conditions that will facilitate this process (Long, 1978, p. 762).

Common and co-operative ownership

Common ownership schemes are distinguished from other forms of financial participation in that the assets are owned collectively and corporately by a majority of the people working in the enterprise. Voting rights are normally proportional to the number of shares held. Such schemes may be distinguished from co-operatives in that voting rights in the latter are normally equally distributed but are not necessarily held by people working in the enterprise. Both however have common origins. They arose from the hardship and struggles imposed on labour by the operation of the market in the nineteenth century, and from attempts to create alternative models for the organisation of production, sometimes by workers themselves, and in other cases by philanthropic entrepreneurs.

There were isolated examples of co-operative production by workers in the eighteenth century but it was not until the growth of the factory system in the nineteenth century that systematic attempts were made to develop worker co-operatives. We noted in Chapter Two the growth of co-operatives in the early decades of the nineteenth century following the repeal of the Combination Acts, and the short-lived attempts to short-circuit the capitalist system of distribution by setting up a series of exchanges. After the failures of the 1830s it was not until the 1850s that there was an attempt to revive producer co-operatives; this time the lead was taken by a group of middle class clergymen and lawyers under the general ideological umbrella of Christian Socialism. The movement started in 1850 and lasted only seven or eight years. Unlike the earlier Owenite movement the Christian Socialists were trying to introduce co-operatives within the working class from outside; nevertheless the Christian Socialist movement, by using its influence within Parliament, both modified the legal system to the benefit of co-operatives and created a positive view of them within some sections of the middle class. The late 1860s and early 1870s saw a re-emergence in a variety of forms of co-operative production but the ensuing depression killed off most of them. There was a resurgence in the 1880s and the number of registered productive societies increased from 15 in 1881 to 120 by the late 1890s. There was a steady decline in numbers thereafter, apart from another brief resurgence of interest at the beginning of the 1920s generated by guild socialism. The decline continued slowly in the inter-war years but in the period after world war two it accelerated considerably (Jones, 1976). The early Owenite notion of co-operatives saw them as a means of establishing new sets of relations of production which would transform capitalist society and abolish private ownership of the means of production. The Christian Socialist tradition which developed in the middle of the nineteenth century saw co-operatives as modifying the nature of capitalist production. From this tradition grew the co-partnership and profit sharing initiatives which continued into the twentieth century.

Since the 1970s there has been a resurgence of interest in, and a renewed growth of, co-operatives in Britain. The government facilitated this trend by the passage of the Common Ownership Act in 1976, which provided limited loan facilities to aid co-operative enterprises; and the setting up of a Co-operative Development Agency in 1978 to promote the establishment and development of co-operative enterprises. The Co-operative Development Agency reported in 1980 that there was a total of 365 co-operatives, of which 175 were in manufacturing and 151 in service industries; of these 85 were in the distribution or retail areas. Approximately one-third of the registered co-operatives existing in 1980 had received help directly or indirectly from the state (Thornley, 1981).

Producer co-operatives existing in Britain today can be broadly divided into three categories. First there are the long established co-operatives which go back to the nineteenth century movement. During the late nineteenth century the Co-operative Productive Federation was the main organiser of producer co-operatives. By 1978 however there were only eight members left in the organisation, largely small firms in the footwear, clothing and printing industries; most of these had a majority of non-worker members, usually drawn from retail co-operatives and the trade unions, and a sizeable section of the workforce with little interest in co-operative principles and unwilling to participate in the running of the organisation.

Second, there are the post-war common ownership firms organised round the Industrial Common Ownership Movement founded in 1958 by Ernest Bader. Bader, a Christian Socialist and the founder of the Scott Bader Commonwealth, had a similar vision to that of his predecessors in the mid-nineteenth century. ICOM encourages only the profits necessary to ensure viability and social benefits for members; the capital of each ICOM firm is considered to be collectively owned and no member can own more than one £1 share; no outside members are permitted. If a firm is wound up then any profits must go to another common ownership firm. 'The rules ensure that each co-operative operates to achieve democratic and other social objectives and does not work in the members' own financial interests or against the expansion of the movement.' (Thornley, 1981, p. 43). There are now 13 full and 70 associated member companies of ICOM; some of these are in catering and distribution. Most are small with under 50 employees. They are largely of two types; first, the companies converted from private ownership, the most well known of which is Scott Bader; second, organisations which derived from the ecological and peace movements and the drive to find alternative ways of living.

The third type of co-operative derives from the response to unemployment in the 1970s and from pressures on public authorities to finance co-operative development as a means of creating jobs or preventing the closure of enterprises. The Manpower Services Commission under its Job Creation Programme, and more recently through its Special Temporary Employment Programme, has funded the setting up of 'enterprise workshops'. These are community projects which aim to provide jobs for the unemployed and to become self-financing within a specific time period. The majority of these have been run as co-operatives or have been working towards co-operative status. By 1980 some 40 co-operative enterprise workshops had been formed of which a quarter had survived to run without government help. Other public funds had been provided for co-operatives through the Scottish and Northern Ireland Development Agencies and through local authorities.

Better known are those co-operatives that were created out of failed conventional business enterprises in order to prevent closure. In most cases workers resisted the initial closure through sit-ins and related tactics and eventually raised capital themselves to buy the enterprise (Elliot, 1978, p. 192). The most celebrated of these are the Kirby Manufacturing and Engineering (KME), Scottish Daily News, and Meriden Motorcycle co-operatives. They owed their existence to large scale government funding and the strong support of Tony Benn, Secretary of State for Industry in 1974-5 (Coates, 1976). These co-operatives were large, undercapitalised, isolated in the market and launched in a glow of — largely hostile — media coverage. They arose out of previous capitalist failure, often after lengthy periods of production disruption, with a co-operative structure which was thrust upon them rather than chosen and of which none of the members had any direct experience (Oakeshott, 1978a, p. 108). Only Meriden now survives.

Producer co-operation is more developed in some other parts of Western Europe than in the United Kingdom. In Italy in 1977 there were 2,675 producer co-operatives and their development is encouraged both by legislation and tax concessions (Oakeshott, 1978a, p. 146). In 1978 in France 556 co-operatives were affiliated to the main co-operative federation, including one organisation with a workforce of nearly four thousand (p. 125). In Spain there has developed over the last 20 years what perhaps has become the best known system of co-operative organisation in Western Europe, the Mondragon co-operatives of northern Spain (Campbell et al., 1977). In the United States, despite substantial co-operative activity at the turn of the century, few such organisations now survive. One small group of longstanding producer co-operatives exists in the plywood manufacturing industry and co-operative organisations also operate in the refuse collecting industry on the west coast (Bellas, 1975; Russell et al., 1979).

Co-operatives and worker participation

Within co-operatives the relationship of workers to ownership, control and participation varies; unfortunately there is very little British research to draw upon in order to examine the nature of these relationships. As we have noted, the traditional co-operatives have a system of ownership not confined only to company employees. At Ideal Clothiers, the 75 year old producer co-operative at Wellingborough, worker directors comprise only one third of directors. They are elected by all worker shareholders; however, as many workers have chosen not to purchase shares, the electorate comprises only 30% of the workforce. In addition, voting is in proportion to share ownership so that not all worker shareholders have equal votes (IRRR, 1975).

Within Scott Bader membership of the Commonwealth (the holding company) is open to all employees over 20 who have completed six months probation and a further one year's employment. There are no outside shareholders. Thirty per cent of employees have elected not to become members and another ten per cent are not eligible. Scott Bader has two main formal organisational levels, the Commonwealth and the operating company. At the Commonwealth level there is a board of management which is responsible for membership of the Commonwealth and acts as custodian of the principles of the Commonwealth. This has six elected members from the Commonwealth and two non-elected members. At the operating company level there is a company board of ten of whom two are elected members. There is also a company council of 15 elected members which approves company board members and their salaries and can make recommendations to the board on any matter related to the running of the company. Slightly aside from this there is a board of seven trustees whose role is to arbitrate between the board and the company council if necessary and also to protect the principles of the Commonwealth. The chairman of the company, who is the son of the founder, is chairman for life.

Participation in the processes of election by those eligible is relatively high, with an 84% poll recorded in 1975 for two vacancies on the board of management, with ten contestants. However, while not invariably the case, there is a strong tendency for deferential voting to take place and for the workforce to elect its managerial members as worker directors on both the company board and the board of management (IRRR, 1975). A similar phenomenon has been noted in relation to other common ownership ventures. The study by Flanders and his colleagues of the John Lewis Partnership indicated that management dominated both the representative functions and the decision-making processes (Flanders, 1968).

There is some evidence therefore from British data that a significant minority of workers in co-operatives do not participate as members. Moreover, amongst co-operative members there is a tendency for managerial workers to be over-represented in the participative and control structures. Edelstein has argued on the basis of a study of four medium sized British worker co-operatives (including the three Tony Benn co-operatives) that there is a 'common tendency for management to become more conventional – that is, more authoritarian and more highly paid – in times of financial crisis...Even dedicated co-operators in management have often argued that the workers' ultimate power to discharge them was enough; that they, the managers, should be allowed to manage without much "interference". Clearly, self management and industrial producers' co-operation are not synonymous.' (Edelstein, 1979, p. 262). For him, this is a reason for retaining unions in co-operatives.

Similar findings come from studies of American co-operatives. Russell and his colleagues report that amongst the refuse collecting co-operatives in San Francisco, whilst there had always been shareholding partners and non-shareholding helpers, non-shareholding helpers had usually expected to become company members after a few years' experience. In recent years however it has become 'common to see Italian-American worker-owners leading crews of black and hispanic workers who have little hope of becoming co-owners. This transformation has had a visible impact on owner/non-owner relationships.' (Russell et al., p. 333). One element of this (in addition to the indications of labour segmentation) has been increasing union activity and the development of normal collective bargaining arrangements. 'Clearly many helpers now see union membership, rather than share ownership, as their best hope for gaining a greater voice in decision-making.' (p. 334). The same authors also note that amongst shareholding partners an initial situation of equal shareholdings, equal authority and equal income has gradually evolved, as a result of growth and technological and economic changes, to one where a managerial elite dominates the boards of directors and the operations of the companies. Nevertheless, 'these firms cannot be dismissed as mere managerial oligarchies. Instead, they appear to be institutions in which the formidable powers of managers are somewhat balanced by the authority of the democratic bodies that elect them.' (p. 333).

Some of these themes are given a further gloss in a study of French co-operatives (Batstone, 1978). It was based on the records of some 60 co-operatives in the Paris region which were broadly representative of the structure of French co-operatives in general, some documentary material on all French co-operatives held by the central agency for co-operative production (SCOP), and detailed case studies of five producer co-operatives. Workers in French co-operatives have the right to become members after working in the co-operative for five years; voting is on the principle of one person – one vote amongst shareholders, but members of the co-operative do not need to be employed by it. Non-employed members are not allowed to hold more than one third of the seats on the board. Overall about one third of employees in the co-operatives are members though this varies by industry with just over a quarter in construction and over 60% in printing. Batstone found that the majority of worker directors were white collar rather than manual workers. This represented a higher tendency for white collar workers to be shareholders in the co-operative; it might also reflect the deferential voting tendency which we noted earlier. In a number of co-operatives however there was a conscious policy of ensuring that the directors came from all sections of the workforce.

Batstone also suggests (though with a number of qualifying caveats) that the participative nature of co-operatives varies over their life cycle. He suggests three phases. In the first phase of 'primitive democracy', at the setting up stage of a co-operative, those involved are highly committed to the co-operative nature of the enterprise. If the co-operative survives it will tend to expand and the pioneering spirit to evaporate amongst the original members; in addition both expansion and natural turnover mean that new workers will be recruited who do not have the idealism of the founder members. There will be a decline in the number of employee members of the co-operative and the development of a more orthodox management function. This is the second phase, of 'professional management'. As new managers take over from the original founder members and as the number of non-member workers increases the original basis of managerial legitimacy becomes weaker. There is a tendency for conventional forms of worker organisation and collective bargaining to develop which form a new but different basis for participation. There is an overall increase in co-operative membership. This is the third stage, of 'representative democracy'. Whilst Batstone puts forward his life cycle model in a tentative fashion he claims that it fits broadly with the data on French co-operatives.

Some further evidence of the relationship between worker ownership and worker participation and control of the enterprise is provided by the increasing number of studies of the Mondragon co-operatives in the Basque region of northern Spain. These are generally held to be an extremely successful instance of co-operative organisation. Indeed Johnson and Whyte have described them as the one important exception to the general rule that co-operatives degenerate (Johnson and Whyte, 1977).

The Mondragon co-operatives now cover a range of activities including farming, education and distribution; the core of the system is made up of industrial enterprises. The first co-operative was established with 23 workers in 1955 and there are now approximately 70. They range in size from Ulgor, the largest with 3,500 employees, to enterprises employing less than 50, and are engaged in a large range of manufacturing activities from washing machines to machine tools. The membership consists of all those working in the enterprise, with no outsiders. Each individual member must make a capital contribution to the enterprise and the workforce as a whole must raise 20% of the initial capital required. Individual ownership stakes are negatively affected by losses as well as positively by profits. The individual share can only be withdrawn on retirement or on leaving the co-operative (when 80% may be withdrawn). Control of the enterprise is formally exercised by the workforce. At an annual general assembly it elects a control board of members (the Junta Rectora) which in turn elects or appoints the chief executive or general manager. 'Once chosen he or she will appoint the subordinate management staff. The top manager will normally enjoy security of tenure in the post for a specific period of years. The only real sanction which the Junta Rectora will hold will be the ultimate one of dismissal. In this way something very like the exercise of normal management functions is protected.' (Oakeshott, 1978b, p. 52).

Strangely, none of the research material on Mondragon indicates the occupational composition of the Junta. Journalistic accounts however suggest that there is a white collar and management bias in its composition. The Junta meets once a month to review management performance. Eaton suggests that this review process is largely illusory. He quotes one worker as telling him: 'the co-operative is a good idea but over the course of time falls into the hands of management and chief executive, who, through having more information and resources than the Junta Rectora can always make their own opinions and points of view prevail' (Eaton, 1979, p. 36). Eaton goes on to argue, in similar terms to those used in the analyses of the role of worker directors on the board of the British Steel Corporation, that 'the workers had no effect on the decision-making process because the Junta Rectora was not where it occurred. Even if it was nothing would change much because the managers have a near-monopoly of knowledge, of the appropriate terminology and of authority, while the members of the Junta are only individuals with no sanctions or power' (p. 36).

Most of the accounts of Mondragon emphasise the high priority placed upon technical and economic efficiency by the co-operatives. The founding members of Mondragon believed that in order to compete with private enterprise they would have to adopt the established methods of management and industrial engineering. Having commented on the freedom of the senior executive to appoint his own management team Johnson and Whyte go on to argue that 'the immediate supervisor may direct his workforce just as autocratically and inflexibly as his counterpart in the private firm. Furthermore, the organisational planners unquestioningly followed the pattern of scientific management in breaking down jobs into simple routine operations and into structuring the workflow into assembly lines. Only one major principle of scientific management was rejected by the system: individual or group piece rates.' (Johnson and Whyte, 1977, p. 25).

The traditional management orientation is reinforced by the Caja Laboral Popular, the co-operative bank which provides 60% of original funding for all new enterprises but also takes a central role in ensuring that the co-operatives are successful in the market. Oakeshott comments that 'at least as important at the Caja's role as a source of capital is the management and consultancy and back-up service provided by its empresarial division, the staff of which numbers about 100. They include a full range of relevant professionals; accountants, engineers, economists, architects, people with experience of industrial management and marketing, and even psychologists. Together with those provisions which protect the management function inside the production co-operatives, it is the empresarial division of the Caja which has enabled the Mondragon co-operatives to solve the other besetting problem with which industrial co-operatives have always had to contend; indequate management. Evidence that the problem has been solved is provided by the extraordinary record of no industrial failures, no bankruptcies – only the one solitary setback over the co-operative fishing boats.' (Oakeshott, 1978b, p. 54).

The protection of the management function has clearly not taken place without generating some strain between management and worker members. In the bigger co-operatives social councils have been set up to allow members to influence managements on matters directly affecting their welfare. The chairman of the social council is the head of the management board and it is composed of representatives from the departments/works units. Its role is advisory to management. In the largest co-operative, Ulgor, Johnson and Whyte found that there was a growing belief amongst members that the social council 'served mainly as a one way channel of communication from management to workers and does not provide a channel by which workers can influence management' (Johnson and Whyte, 1977, p. 25). In 1974 there was a dispute over job evaluation at Ulgor. The protestors refused to use the social council as an agreement channel, seeing it as ineffectual and weak, and they went on strike. The strike was short lived. Management have been trying since then to find ways of increasing workers' direct participation in work organisation through job restructuring. The larger Mondragon co-operatives, as they have grown and developed, have encountered the fundamental difficulty of reconciling scientific management techniques, seen as necessary for effective production, with the basic co-operative ethos. 'This contradiction provides scope for a possible trade union consciousness amongst shopfloor co-operative members. There are some anxieties amongst management about trade union penetration and even now such worries may not be groundless at Ulgor and Copreci, the larger co-operatives.' (Eaton, 1979, p. 40).

The self-managed economy

The tensions between ownership and control which appear in studies of worker co-operatives within capitalist organisations are also evident within the self-managed economy. Yugoslavia provides both the best example and the richest source of research material on the self-managed enterprise in the self-managed economy.

In the period immediately following the second world war Yugoslavia had a centrally planned economy managed by the State on the same pattern as other Soviet bloc countries. Yugoslavia broke away from the Soviet Union in 1948 and was expelled from the Cominform. The sudden disappearance of an export market, a source of imports, and a source of capital, coupled with political and military tension, brought chaos to the Yugoslav economy. At the same time the break from the Soviet Union meant that the Soviet model of a centrally planned socialist economy was no longer *de rigeur* and there was an urgent need to mobilise the energies of both political activists and workers in order to salvage the economy. Gradually between 1948 and 1953 the notion of a self-managed economy was evolved in discussion, debate and practice. Workers' councils were introduced into industrial enterprises, initially as advisory and consultative bodies, from 1949; in 1952 the control of all state enterprises was formally vested in workers' councils, and the 1953 constitution gave self-management a legal and constitutional basis.

The Yugoslav self-management system developed in the direction of giving increasing autonomy to the enterprise. By the mid-sixties, although significant progress had been made towards a decentralised self-managed system, 'there continued to be a large degree of central control of the economy and particularly of investment, in the interests of co-ordination and stabilisation or ensuring what was termed the "basic proportions" of development' (Dubey, 1975). A new basic law in 1965 gave increased freedom to the enterprise, and an amendment to the constitution in 1969 gave enterprises freedom to create their own self-management structures;

the only structural legal requirement was the establishment of a workers' council.

By the end of the sixties the basic elements of the self-management system were as follows. A workers' council is elected by a workers' assembly consisting of all members of the enterprise. The workers' council members are elected for two years with half of the membership re-elected every year; the council in turn elects a management board which acts as its executive agent. The council has responsibility for all decisions concerning the running of the enterprise. No one can be elected twice in succession to the workers' council or more than twice in succession to the management board; the chairman of the council cannot be a member of the board. The workers' council has to meet not less than once every six weeks; its meetings are attended by the management board and may be attended by interested workers, and representatives of the trade union and the League of Communists' organisation in the plant. The enterprise is administered on a day to day basis by a director and management team. Recommendations for filling the post of director and the selection of candidates are undertaken by a committee, half of whom are appointed by the workers' council, half by the local community council; the workers' council however is responsible for the decision to appoint. The director is appointed for four years with the possibility of re-appointment for an additional term. The director cannot be a member of the workers' council. The workers' council has the right to remove the director before his term of office has expired, for breaches of the law, incompetence, or when the enterprise cannot meet its financial obligations.

The enterprise in Yugoslavia is defined as social property; workers in it are entitled to manage it but not to own it. If the enterprise is successful then its total income is distributed in a number of ways. After the deduction of operating expenses, and sums for depreciation and contractual obligations, a percentage of profit is paid out in federal, republic, and communal taxes. Over the period of development of the self-management system the proportion of profit going to these taxes (and therefore the proportion available for the enterprise) has varied from 80% in the early days to a current norm of about 30%. Workers in the enterprise are paid a basic wage and of the remaining profit the workers' council decides what amount to reinvest in the firm, what amount to distribute to the workforce, and what amount to spend on collective consumption projects such as new housing. If the enterprise does not make a profit workers must still get 66% of their average salaries; if the enterprise cannot pay this from its reserves then the community has to furnish funds for a limited period whilst its future is decided.

There have been a number of studies of participation and decision-making in the Yugoslav self-managed enterprise. Kolaja in his study of two Yugoslav factories in 1959 concluded that 'the major functions of both workers' councils as I observed them, was information and education.

Management was informed by worker members of the council about the attitudes of the rank and file, and worker members were exposed to managerial problems...In both enterprises management got all the measures in which it was interested accepted by the workers' council.' (Kolaja, 1965, p. 77). Rus synthesised seven studies on the distribution of influence in the enterprise and concluded that in all seven situations, influence over decision-making was perceived as being concentrated in the top management structure (Rus, 1970).

Obrodovic complemented these studies of perceived participation by gathering, from observational studies, behavioural data on actual participation in workers' councils in 20 enterprises. According to Yugoslav law top managers are prohibited from being members of workers' councils but Obrodovic found 17 top managers in his sample of companies who were members of workers' councils. However, workers' council meetings are open and it is legal for top managers to attend and speak. Obrodovic's data indicated that 'top management plays a major role in all stages of the councils' deliberations, although this is less so at the decision-making stage (acceptance and rejection of a proposal) than in explanations and discussions. In particular, top management generally participated most often, interacted most often, and for the greatest length of time, offered the most proposals, and have the most proposals accepted. Further, they tended to talk longer each time they spoke...indicating that their major role was defining proposals.' (Obrodovic, 1975, p. 37). Level of education and membership of the League of Communists were also highly correlated with intensity of participation, but both these categories overlapped to a high degree with being a manager. Obrodovic does suggest that there is a higher degree of participation by lower level workers in discussion of 'human relations problems at the individual and group level, standard of living and social welfare issues and hiring and placement problems' (p. 46).

A number of considerations have been put forward to explain the paradox that whilst workers' councils were set up to appoint and control management, management in fact controls the workers' councils. Management through their function in the organisation acquire a wide range of knowledge and information which is fundamental to the issues which come up at the workers' council. They can filter and decide on the mode and timing of distribution and presentation of information. Part of that presentation will take place in the context of shared meanings, understandings and vocabularies which reduce the effective participation of those workers who lack access to them. 'Equally as important has been management's necessary and often automatic access to and close links with influential social actors in other spheres (local politicians, party leaders etc.) and higher level institutions (federal and republic planners and inspectors, bankers). This provides managers and technicians with informational advantages as well as external persons and arguments which they can refer to in legitimising their choices and decisions. They have also the possibility of calling on these persons and organisations through party, trade unions, and government channels, to influence the opinions and judgements of enterprise workers.' (Baumgartner et al., 1979, p. 101).

Further evidence of the dominance of management cadres in the self-management system is provided by figures on the composition of the workers' council and the management board. Between 1956 and 1972, whilst the proportion of semi- and unskilled workers in the Yugoslav labour force remained approximately constant at 43%, their membership of workers' councils dropped from 24% to 16%, and of the management board from 15% to six per cent. In contrast, whilst the highest grade non-manual working group increased from 3.2% in 1956 to 4.3% of the labour force in 1972 their representation on workers' councils changed over the same period from 3.5% to 11.6% and on management boards from 8.1% to 25.3% (Baumgartner et al., 1979, p. 100). It is important to acknowledge that the Yugoslav system nevertheless gives a remarkable number of persons the opportunity to hold office. Blumberg has calculated that in the first ten years of the self-management system about a quarter of the industrial labour force served on workers' councils and management boards (Blumberg, 1968, p. 215).

In the early days of self-management the aims of the system were to decentralise formal bureaucratic power and to nurture local enterprise control. The directors of enterprises gradually ceased to be state appointees and eventually became appointees of the workers' council. Brannen and his colleagues have suggested that 'whilst the authority of the enterprise director and his management team declined considerably in the early days of self-management the gradual extension of the market principle has led to a re-emergence of that authority. The paradox of the introduction of the market principle into the Yugoslav economy is that whilst it has devolved power within the context of the total society by giving autonomy to the enterprise in relation to the state it has strengthened the movement towards hierarchical government within the enterprise.' (Brannen et al., 1976, p. 227). The increasing autonomy in enterprises from the mid-sixties led to relatively rapid growth and substantial increases in personal income. It also led to increasing variation in standards of living and life chances between social groups, and uneven development between enterprises and regions (Commisso, 1979). General problems of social co-ordination and integration came to the fore.

As a result of these developments there have been a number of attempts at restructuring the management system. The aim has been to increase worker influence, particularly that of the unskilled and semi-skilled, and to limit that of management. This has been done through increasing the formal power of workers in subunits in the enterprise (basic organisations of associated labour), increasing the power of the workers' councils and giving workers access to specialised units providing accounting, financial analysis, and other services. There has also, however, been a move back towards centralising control. The autonomy of the enterprise has been restricted by creating a new range of intermediate institutions to co-ordinate and regulate the actions and interests of enterprises. Introduced through the 1974 constitution they are intended to serve as a self-managed planning system. The reforms seem to have had little effect in creating greater economic stability or equality (ibid.). At the level of the enterprise there continued to be evidence of low involvement by ordinary workers in the business decision of the enterprise. Commisso however puts forward a positive view of this: the 'low participation rate of non-supervisory personnel in business policy decisions at Klek [a Zagreb machine tool plant] was less a sign of alienation and powerlessness than a sign of consensus on management's goals and confidence in its intentions and ability to protect the collective's best interests' (p. 190). A system perhaps of self management by exception!

Conclusion

The last chapter ended with the proposition put forward by an economic commentator, that the solution to the economic problems of the market system was to move towards a general system of workers' co-operatives (Jay, 1977). Part of the logic of this proposal was that it would 'put collective bargaining to sleep'. It has been criticised on the grounds that it would simply transform conflict between employers and workers into a different type of conflict, between finance capital (which would remain in private hands in Jay's proposal) and industrial management. 'While ostensibly a system of workers' co-operatives, it would really be one of labour only sub-contracting by financial capital through the economy.' (Crouch, 1978, p. 239).

The evidence presented in this chapter would suggest on the contrary that the presumed integration between labour and management which is the *raison d'être* behind Jay's proposal is itself not self-evident. The main thrust of the chapter has been to show that there is no clear relationship between economic democracy, that is the communal ownership of the means of production, and workers' participation in and control over the running of the enterprise. There have been several strands to the discussion. First, economic democracy or sub-economic democracy has no necessary relationship to workers' participation. The fact of being an owner does not have any implications of itself for participation at the socio-technical level or the political level of enterprise control. In the case of Mondragon, for example, the application of scientific management techniques is a deliberate strategy for ensuring that the co-owners exercise no control at the task and work group levels.

In many instances, as we have seen, co-operatives have non-member workers and 'have become, in effect, associations of capitalists, ... making profit for themselves by the employment at wages of workers outside their association' (S. and B. Webb, 1920). But even within the membership of co-operatives, there is a tendency for white collar and management groups to dominate the representative institutions, and for these institutions themselves to be dominated by the managers they appoint. There is a constant tendency for the hierarchical and authority system to reassert itself and for conflict to develop between it and the object of its authority. These tensions arise out of the operations of the market and the technology of production. Nevertheless there is also some evidence that economic democracy creates a greater attachment of workers to the organisation and that the ability of the workforce to employ capital and management does much to convert 'power bargaining based on distrust into problem solving based on trust' (Fox, 1974, p. 358). Conflict generated out of the production and market processes will not disappear: it is the context for their resolution which is different. We will return to these themes in the concluding chapter.

Further Reading

Material on employee share ownership in Britain is not extensive. See however White (1980), Bell (1980) and Creigh et al. (1981). Lodge and Henderson (1979) and Metzger (1981) provide general information on the United States, and detailed studies are provided by Conte and Tanenbaum (1978) and Long (1978). A good general source of information is Latta (1979). Elvander (1979) provides a discussion of the Meidner proposals. A useful background text on co-operative ownership is Derrick and Phipps (1969). For more recent accounts see Oakeshott (1978a) and Thornley (1981). There is a large literature on Yugoslavia; Blumberg (1969) provides a useful, though dated, introductory account; Wachtel (1973) and Commisso (1979) are more recent sources; see also Baumgartner et al. (1979).

9 · Conclusion

In this book we have tried to cover a broad canvas, showing the variety of issues involved in the topic of worker participation, and to indicate connections between some of these issues. This concluding chapter takes a synoptic view of some of these connections. In the introduction we set out a number of dimensions of participation which could act as benchmarks in subsequent discussion. Essentially the subject is concerned with the exercise of worker power or control at a variety of levels in and over the operation of the enterprise. The ownership of the means of production and administration provides the highest level of control within industrial society; participation at this level we termed economic participation. In addition to control over the means of production it is also possible to conceive of control in relation to managerial policies, that is control at the political level of the enterprise, and control over conditions of employment and work organisation, that is control at the socio-technical level of the enterprise. The participation of workers can be exercised in relation to each of these levels of control in a full or a partial way. It is possible to have full or partial participation at one level without having any participation at other levels. Formal rights of participation, which may be thought of as industrial citizenship, may be conferred by the State through law or they may be obtained by agreements within industry – between the workforce and its agents and the owners (who may be the State or indeed the workforce itself as well as capital) and their agents. The relationship between formal rights and actual practice, however, is problematic; also, control can be exercised without formal rights.

Our focus has been on worker participation within market society. We have not explored in this book the relationships of labour to the economy in societies where there is complete State ownership and control of the means of production and where formal planning mechanisms, rather than the market, guide development. There are however a wide variety of institutional forms of workers' participation, operating in different market societies at different levels of the enterprise. Within each society the origins of the institutional form, its relationship to the wider socio-economic context, the processes that go on within it and their evaluation by different groups of actors, its coverage in terms of occupational groups, and the degree to which it operates to increase the control exercised by these groups, will differ. So also will the amount of research undertaken into each institutional form and the conclusions of that research. Quite often the degree of participation which takes place is more dependent on the context in which the institution operates than the nature of the institution itself.

It is for these reasons that, whilst we have looked at some forms of participation in a number of countries, the book has largely concentrated on Britain. In doing so it has highlighted a number of dimensions that are important to an understanding of the development and practice of worker participation. These include: structural factors, such as economic and technical conditions; cultural factors, such as the orientations and ideologies of management, labour, and State; and institutional factors such as the arrangements for organising the interaction between labour and management. These elements provide the framework within which the potential for participation of a variety of categories of social actors may be understood, and also their inclination or propensity to participate and the processes of such participation. The relationship of these elements to each other will however vary over time and at different points in the economy. So while the dimensions that are to be examined are the same in each country, their interactions are in part unique, and the institutions that arise and the outcomes of the process within these institutions may differ. Thus, for the purposes of this text it was felt to be more useful to examine these dimensions mainly against the background of one country rather than attempting a broad comparative analysis. This is not to argue that at a conceptual level such an analysis is not possible or that there have not been interesting examples (see Poole, 1981) or useful attempts to move beyond comparative institutional description (IDE, 1981). Equally, there has been some apparent convergence of findings in the outcomes from particular institutional forms across societies (Brannen et al., 1976, pp. 245-64; Batstone and Davies, 1976).

In looking at the development of both industrial citizenship and participation in Britain we saw how they had emerged from the exercise of collective power through both the political process and industrial action. We also saw that institutional forms become weak and often disappear once collective power wanes through changes in external market circumstances. Marx's analysis of industrial capitalism suggested that there would be constant pressure to rationalise the processes of production in order to increase surplus value. This could be done through producing more output from labour by intensifying work effort or through increasing productivity by introducing new technology. Braverman also saw the process of capitalist development as one of deskilling, in which the workers' control over the processes of production has been constantly subverted. There are clear signs that this has happened, and not only within capitalist enterprises or capitalist economies. But alongside this there have also been other processes at work. The changing nature of industrial production has led to the concentration and centralisation of capital. Concentration is associated with growth in trade union membership; it also means that labour is able to impose increasing costs on capital. Workers themselves have, through the political system, through collective powers, and through individual and group manipulation of the processes of work organisation, sought both to resist managerial control and to exert control themselves over the production process. In order to secure the co-operation of the workforce in maximising output, and to deal with the conflict that arises out of simply treating labour as a factor of production, managements within industrial market society have themselves sought means of attaching workers to the firm and of institutionalising conflict. Both labour and capital have sought, in other words, to adapt the relations of production to changes in the means of production.

We have seen that historically there have been a number of periods when there were waves of interest in participation and new institutional growth; in particular this occurred in the first two decades of this century, the period around the second world war, and from the mid-1960s until the late 1970s. This pattern has not simply been typical of Britain but also of a number of other market economies, although the institutional reaction has varied (Sorge, 1974, pp. 286-7). Participation becomes important during periods of crisis in which labour is in short supply, and it is important for employers and for the State to keep output high, but when also for a variety of reasons increases in money wages are difficult. These conditions aid the bargaining power of labour but wage restraint blocks traditional money-based demands and the pressure for increased output and efficiency focuses attention on issues in the sphere of production. Within these situations participation comes to be seen as an alleviation of strain in the relationships of production, by management, workers and government. Each group is affected differently, however, and does not necessarily act to achieve similar goals.

Crises are by definition relatively short-term. When the move is from crisis to slump then the industrial power of workers is reduced while at the same time the employer is more ready to engage in confrontation with the workforce. When the move is in the opposite direction then market and political pressures on wage restraint are lessened and employers and government are more willing to concede wage demands. Trade union and worker demands have generally related to distributional issues over most of the period of industrialisation. In periods of boom the institutions of wage bargaining are revitalised and the other institutions of participation fall into disfavour.

The history of industrial Britain is one in which there has been a relatively steady growth of formal institutions of industrial relations; this has taken place however against a changing and discontinuous pattern of industrial conflict involving attempts to modify the pattern of industrial authority. Although interest in participation has tended to decline once a crisis has passed, the situation does not revert back to the pre-crisis position. Some remnants of the institutions linger on to be revived at the next wave; others continue to develop and grow in particular sectors although often against resistance from either management or unions. Workforce expectations for industrial citizenship rights increase over time; demand within the system grows and parameters of managerial authority are subject to increasing challenge. Resistance to this challenge risks desubordination and destabilisation. It was suggested in Chapter Seven that inflation over the last two decades can be thought of as one aspect of this.

A number of commentators have argued that pressures for participation linked to changes in the economic cycle are common to a variety of market societies. The explanation for waves of participation based on economic cycles is limited however in that it does not explain the different forms which emerge and are established in specific market societies (Poole, 1981, p. 25). In addition there is disagreement over whether, since the most recent wave of interest, we are now moving into an evolutionary phase in the development of participative institutions or whether the cycles will continue (Poole, 1982; Ramsey, 1983). Let us now examine this issue in the light of the material presented in the middle sections of the book and likely trends in the 1980s.

It is important not to over-emphasise the extent or degree of pressure for participation even during waves of interest. There are also strong counter-pressures. We have seen in Chapter Four that within the workforce during the most recent wave, whilst there was a general demand for some increase in participation, the major focus was at the socio-technical level; there was little demand for participation at the political level of the enterprise and almost none for economic democracy other than forms of financial participation. In the workforce there is of course a diversity of work orientations and work situations that lead to a differential potential for and propensity to participate. The workforce has a variety of ways of viewing work stemming from structural and historical factors within the work situation and bio-social and community factors outside it. Most of the studies undertaken of worker participation have been amongst workers in the primary sectors of the labour force. These workforces are by definition highly unionised and have the highest potential for participation. Most of them however expressed no wish to challenge management's right to manage, but simply wished to influence the operation of that right; collective bargaining was seen as the most effective way of exerting that influence.

The trade unions and their full-time officials have also been generally hostile to participation at both the political and socio-technical levels of the enterprise. Like other organisations trade unions have formal goals which are more or less clearly articulated and which are pursued to a greater or lesser extent by their officials. We have seen in earlier chapters how the main interests of British unions historically have been in the protection of pay and conditions for their members and the main means of achieving this has been seen as collective bargaining. Michels argued that permanent union officials, once appointed, would inevitably dominate rank and file members, in part because they have superior access to and control of information, channels of communication, and political resources, and in part because of membership ignorance and apathy. He also argued that officials once appointed would develop their own organisational interests which would be distant from and could even be opposed to membership interests (Michels, 1962). A number of studies have produced support for this thesis (eg Lipset et al., 1956); others have suggested that, by and large, union officials pursue members' interests if only to retain membership and their own power (Allen, 1954). Jackson has recently argued that union leaders are concerned to protect their own position and normally act in a conservative fashion. They will however, because of this, respond to any widespread membership demands (Jackson, 1982). We have seen in earlier chapters how economism is the major element in worker orientation. We have also seen how formal trade union organisations in Britain have been wary of entering into forms of worker participation outside the traditional collective bargaining mode. In one sense this might be seen as reflecting both the organisational conservatism of trade union leaders and members' interests. However, the forms of worker participation which are work-based or company-based might also be seen to extend the power and authority of trade union members and their lay representatives within the company and to diminish that of full-time officials.

The issue of worker participation has largely been treated in this book as one of control. There is however also an issue of representation, that is of the distribution of control within the workforce between different groups of workers. At one level this can be seen simply as a mechanical issue related to the composition of the representatives in various committees by occupation or union; this was the case in much of the post-Bullock dabate. The issue referred to here though is the broader one of who participates. The labour market, as we noted in Chapter Four, is segmented and workers within it have differentiated market power. Secondary segments are characterised by various combinations of low pay, insecurity, lack of training and career structures, and low unionisation; some secondary segments are made up of small firms, others exist as enclaves in larger firms. Workers in these segments lack the negative protection against exploitation provided by trade unions; often they also lack the the positive protection of law since, because of work instability, they will often not have the required length of service for legal protection. Some form of organisation is an essential element in participation as also is some form of knowledge and understanding. The conditions for these, stability and cohesion, are lacking in these secondary segments of the labour market. Moreover, unstable, low paid employment operates to create sets of work attitudes and orientations which are negative in relation to participation.

It is often argued that workers' lack of interest in participation and of education for it are sufficient reasons for opposing any extension. It could equally be claimed that opportunity creates potential. Historically, though in a gradual way, the appetite for participation has grown amongst the workforce as experience of it has spread. In addition there is some evidence that skilled workers and shop stewards, both of whom in different ways exercise control in the work situation, are more positively oriented towards increasing participation than other categories of workers. According to Pateman, 'the evidence suggests that the low existing level of demand for high level participation in the work place might, at least in part, be explained as an effect of the socialisation process which, both through the notion of his role-to-be at work gained by the ordinary boy [*sic*] and through the experiences of the individual inside the work place, could lead to the idea of higher level participation being "unavailable" for many workers.' (Pateman, 1970, p. 107). Attitudes arise from and are constructed within particular situations.

Some evidence for this interest is also apparent in the attitudes of management towards various forms of participation. As we have seen in Chapters Five and Six there is a high degree of hostility amongst management towards participation at the political level of the enterprise; where schemes of this kind have been introduced, on the other hand, attitudes have become more positive. Nevertheless, by and large management attitudes towards participation are the mirror image of those of ordinary employees, with regard to the level at which it is perceived that there is scope for activity. For managment as for ordinary employees the socio-technical level is seen as the relevant one. However, the type of activity which management defines as participatory differs from that defined by the workforce. Management's definition tends maximally to relate to consultation, minimally to the upwards or downwards flow of information; that is, management are interested in partial participation or in what Pateman called 'pseudo participation'. By contrast the workforce, albeit in restricted areas, tends to aspire to partial or full participation.

Management are resistant to full participation because they see it as threatening their authority and control. They clearly have a vested interest in maintaining these; but in addition they are firmly of the view that economic efficiency demands hierarchy and authority. In that they echo Weber's analysis of the needs of modern industrial society. Weber, it will be recollected, argued that the formal rationality of capitalism led necessarily to a division of labour based on authority and hierarchy. The evidence, however, suggests that schemes of participation, whether they have been at the socio-technical level or the political level, within the capitalist firm, the self managed firm or the self managed market economy, do not interfere with efficiency. One reason for this is that the market creates pressures which ensure managerial control independently of the system of ownership. Another is that efficiency, other than within a totalitarian context, requires some accommodation with worker interests. So, for example, the historical dominance of pay and conditions in workers' interests and its articulation in collective bargaining have been largely and over a long period of time accepted by management, though even here the degree of acceptance is in some respects conditional and fragile.

Social and economic systems change only slowly and there is a large cultural, political and economic investment in the *status quo*. The renewed growth of interest in participation in the period starting in the mid-sixties was due to changes in market, technological, institutional and cultural factors. Whilst it led to some institutional changes and a high volume of public discussion it is clear that the degree of normative commitment by both labour and management was limited, even in a market context that was favourable. The boom that characterised the Western market economies in the post-war period had begun to disappear by the mid-1970s. By the end of the decade these economies had moved into a deep recession the like of which was almost unimaginable a decade earlier. Growth was non-existent, output stagnated and firms closed. Unemployment rose to above 12% of the working population in Britain. The reasons for this major recession do not concern us here but, according to many commentators, it is unlikely to disappear by the end of the decade. Moreover, it has taken place at a time when technological innovation in the shape of the micro-processor is transforming the industrial world in the way electricity did a century ago. Whilst the consequences for the size of employment are unknown (though a number of commentators are pessimistic), this is clearly going to have a major effect on the composition of employment. Combined with its distant cousin, robotics, it seems likely to have the effect of decreasing production jobs and increasing jobs in design, development, sales and maintenance. Office occupations may well also decrease. The proportion of manual jobs will certainly do so. The factory employing very large numbers of people, which was important for traditional assembly line industry, may well become less common. Linked with telecommunications improvements the large head office also may no longer be necessary; a decentralised, small unit system becomes possible.

The consequences of these trends for participation may be set out as follows. Apart from the large numbers of workers not in employment one response of employers to recession is to move work into secondary segments of the market where costs are subject to less regulation. Some primary sector segments therefore shrink and the relative size of some secondary segments grows. The effect of this is that within the primary segments of the labour market the relative power of labour and capital changes. The trade unions lose membership and their bargaining power decreases; in addition their priorities become focused on the saving of jobs and the protection of pay. There is a switch in labour market power back towards management and as a consequence a reassertion of managerial prerogative. Participative structures are a constraint on management flexibility; during recession they are not needed as an incentive or lubricant to the system. We are therefore back in the non-participative phase of the economic cycle.

The above picture is oversimplified. The decline in trade union membership is likely to be concentrated amongst traditional manual unions and there may be some increase in the white collar, technical, and managerial sections of the trade union movement. In recession there are variations in experience between firms. In some firms labour will still be powerful, in others management will be looking for ways of motivating labour other than through pay; in others again the help of the labour force will be required and indeed some sacrifices will be asked for in order to stave off the worst effects of the recession. There may be the need for some co-operation in the face of adversity. As we have seen in Chapter Three there was evidence of an increase in the extent of joint consultation even as the recession began to bite. Moreover, changes in economy and technology do not have a rapid effect on industrial culture. The increase in industrial citizenship which has been evolving over the course of the century cannot suddenly be switched off. Expectations of affluence may be diminished but within a recession awareness increases, though in an inchoate way, of wider issues of control. Though Bullock is dead the issues raised have a sharper meaning in recession. The general level of education and training in the workforce continues to increase and the middle cadres of the workforce are those socialised during the post-war period.

The State in Britain has responded to the economic crisis through the application of a strong market philosophy. This has also happened in a number of other industrialised countries. We have written earlier that the case against workers' participation in terms of efficiency, conceived other than in the narrowest and most short-term way, is by no means self-evident. Within a complex society, too, the State can only work through the co-operation of a variety of groups to achieve its economic goals. It is unlikely, as Jay has argued, that the market can be deinstitutionalised (Jay, 1977b). It is also the case that those Western European countries which have coped best with the recession have been those with the most participative of industrial systems. Within Britain the economic argument for increasing worker participation continues to be perceived as salient within the political system even in a period of deep recession. The Labour Party have introduced a policy document significantly entitled 'Economic Planning and Industrial Democracy', which its employment spokesman has argued is important because 'more industrial democracy is an economic as well as moral and human necessity' (Radice, 1982). The Social Democratic Party has also stated in a policy document that participation is important for reasons of economic efficiency (SDP, 1982).

In July 1982 the Liberal party spokesman on employment in the House of Lords moved an amendment to the Employment Bill, which became incorporated into the Employment Act, making it mandatory on all companies employing more than 250 employees to include in their annual report a statement of steps taken by them to inform and consult employees about a number of aspects of company activities. A Bill covering similar ground had been introduced into Parliament earlier in the year by a number of Conservative MPs but had not proceeded. This Bill was seen by its sponsors as a preliminary step before the introduction of a code of practice on employee participation (Bulmer, 1982). All four main political parties therefore seem committed, though in different ways, to the view that the State should take some action in relation to worker participation.

The situation we have described lends itself to no easy analysis. It seems possible to argue that institutional momentum for increased participation, expressed in the notion of industrial citizenship, has not been arrested by the current recession. Within Britain this expansion and the continuation of interest at the political level indicates a gradual cultural change, which at one and the same time expresses the notion that labour cannot be treated as commodity and that to gain legitimacy, both for national economic management and for the management of the enterprise, there has to be continuing modification of the system of industrial authority. This increasing cultural awareness is fragmented both in its expression and its application. Whilst it recognises that a new normative order within industry is economically necessary and socially desirable, there is still a deeply entrenched commitment by both management and labour to the *status quo* and a reluctance by the State fully to commit itself to the emergent culture. The expansion of participation therefore is fragmented and limited in terms of levels. It is predominantly at the socio-technical level, is partial rather than full, and has a limited impact on the authority structure of the enterprise. In the long term a more coherent and forceful governmental approach to worker participation might emerge. Whatever the role of the State in encouraging worker participation however, legislation only provides a framework. Within that framework issues of management, union and worker orientation, labour market segmentation, and relative market power will still persist.

Goldthorpe has argued that within the British context it is unrealistic to look for solutions to problems in the industrial relations system whilst there is still massive inequality within the wider social system (Goldthorpe, 1974). One source and major element of this inequality lies in the ownership of the means of production. In firms, sectors and societies where there is equality in this and where labour hires capital rather than the reverse there appears to be more social cohesion than within capitalist enterprises. We have seen how Marx understood the private ownership of the means of production to be a central cause of work alienation. When labour is bought by capital there is no control over the product it produces or over the productive task itself; work becomes instrumental and this contributes to the wider alienation of man from his own species being. It is clear however that this analysis is far too simple. Even when the means of production are socially owned man can still be alienated and without control over the work process or a finished product. Within a co-operative system like Mondragon, or a self managed system as in Yugoslavia, there are market pressures which divide the worker from the product of his or her labour and technological pressures to fragment the productive task. This is not to argue that the social ownership of the means of production does not have some effect on 'market alienation'; but it has no necessary effect on 'technological alienation'.

We can look at this from another angle by reverting to Durkheim's analysis of the two main pathologies affecting the division of labour in industrial society. The anomic division of labour, which is similar in many ways to 'technological alienation', was seen by Durkheim as being caused by a lack of connecton between worker and finished product and between consumer and producer. The forced division of labour was created by unequal access to positions of ownership and control. The consequences of these two pathologies was both conflict and social fragmentation. Pressures towards participation are conceived of as arising out of attempts to solve these. However, the abolition of the forced division of labour does not solve the problem of the anomic division of labour. Attack on two separate fronts is required. Whilst Marx saw the detailed division of labour as being related to the capitalist mode of production and the solution to alienation as therefore lying in the abolition of the division of labour, Durkheim accepted the inevitability of the latter and proposed that the solution lay in binding workers into the collective effort. The abolition of the forced division of labour was a necessary but not sufficient condition for this.

In the capitalist firm the functions of co-ordination and control are hierarchically combined, related to the authority and power stemming from the ownership of the means of production and bolstered by the system of stratification in the wider society. Efficiency does not however demand that the systems of co-ordination and control should be combined in this way. Abell has argued, as we saw in the first chapter, that the structuring of the control function might be arrived at independently of the co-ordination function through a system of 'rational democratic authority' (Abell, 1979). This would be based on the political equality of each individual in the organisation, which members could choose to surrender in whole or in part to representatives. They could also choose to recognise that certain decisions were technical and could only be made by those with the relevant competence. Finally, they could choose if they wished to recognise what Abell calls 'the principle of efficiency', that is, that the organisation is there to fulfil certain specified goals. This is essentially the system that operates in Mondragon and in Yugoslavia, and as we have seen in the last chapter there are strong tendencies in both these cases for the co-ordination and control systems to recombine, even at the political level of the organisation.

Economic democracy does not guarantee industrial democracy nor any level of worker participation. It is related but separate; nor within the capitalist system does industrial democracy guarantee participation of a full or partial kind at the level of the socio-technical system. The barriers to both economic and industrial democracy are very great and are deep-rooted in our society. There are no clear ways forward. It has been the aim of this book to set out some of the evidence and available analysis in the hope that it will encourage others to engage in research which might help to unblock and resolve one of the major issues of the late twentieth century.

Bibliography

ABELL, P., (1979), 'Hierarchy and Democratic Authority', in BURNS, TOM, R., LARS ERIK KARLSSON and VELJKO RUS, (eds.), *Work and Power – The Liberation of Work and the Control of Political Power*, Sage, 1979.

ABRAHAMSSON, BENGT, (1977), *Bureaucracy or Participation*, Sage.

ALBROW, MARTIN, (1970), *Bureaucracy*, Macmillan.

ALLEN, V. L., (1954), *Power in Trade Unions*, Longman.

ALLEN, V. L., (1971), *The Sociology of Industrial Relations*, Longman.

BALFOUR, CAMPBELL, (1973), *Participation in Industry*, Croom Helm.

BANK, JOHN and KEN JONES, (1977), *Worker-Directors Speak*, Farnborough, Gower Press.

BATSTONE, ERIC, (1978), *The Organisation and Behaviour of French Co-operatives*, (unpublished).

BATSTONE, ERIC, (1979), Systems of Domination, Accommodation and Industrial Democracy', in TOM R. BURNS, LARS ERIC KARLSSON and VELJKO RUS (eds.), *Work and Power – The Liberation of Work and the Control of Political Power*, Sage.

BATSTONE, ERIC, and P. L. DAVIES, (1976), *Industrial Democracy: European Experience*, HMSO.

BATSTONE, ERIC, ANTHONY FERNER and MICHAEL TERRY, (1983), *Unions at the Board – A Case Study of Industrial Democracy in the Post Office, 1978-1979*, Oxford, Blackwell.

BAUMGARTNER, TOM, TOM R. BURNS and DUSKO SEKULIC, (1979), 'Self-Management, Market, and Political Institutions in Conflict: Yugoslav Development Patterns and Dialectics', in TOM R. BURNS, LARS ERIC KARLSSON and VELJKO RUS (eds.), *Work and Power – The Liberation of Work and the Control of Political Power*, Sage.

BEAUMONT, P. and D. R. DEATON, (1981), 'The Extent and Determinants of Joint Consultative Arrangements in Britain', *Journal of Management Studies*, Vol. 18, no. 1, pp. 49-71.

BELL, D. WALLACE, (1980), *Profit Sharing and Employee Shareholding Report*, Industrial Participation Association.

BELLAS, C. J., (1975), 'Industrial Democracy through Worker Ownership: An American Experience', in JAROSLAV VANEK (ed.), *Self Management: Economic Liberation of Man*, Penguin.

BENDIX, REINHARD, (1974), *Work and Authority in Industry*, University of California Press.

BERG, I., M. FREEDMAN and M. FREEMAN, (1978), *Managers and Work Reform: a Limited Engagement,* New York, Free Press.

BERLE, A. A. and G. C. MEANS, (1932), *The Modern Corporation and Private Property,* Macmillan.

BEYNON, H. and R. M. BLACKBURN, (1972), *Perceptions of Work,* Cambridge University Press.

BIM, (1968), *Industrial Democracy,* Occasional Paper No. 1, British Institute of Management.

BIM, (1977), *Employee Participation — the Way Ahead,* British Institute of Management.

BLACKBURN, R. M. and M. MANN, (1979), *The Working Class in the Labour Market,* Macmillan.

BLAUNER, ROBERT, (1967), *Alienation and Freedom,* University of Chicago Press.

BLUMBERG, PAUL, (1968), *Industrial Democracy: The Sociology of Participation,* Constable.

BOSANQUET, M. and P. B. DOERINGER, (1973), 'Is There a Dual Labour Market in Great Britain?', *Economic Journal,* 83, pp. 421-35.

BRANNEN, PETER, ERIC BATSTONE, DEREK FATCHETT, PHILIP WHITE, (1971), *Employee Participation in the British Steel Corporation with Special Reference to the Employee Director Scheme,* Report to BSC and the Steel Committee of the TUC.

BRANNEN, PETER, and J. E. T. ELDRIDGE, (1973), *Employee Participation in The British Steel Corporation,* Report to the Social Science Research Council.

BRANNEN, PETER, (1975), *Entering the World of Work: Some Sociological Perspectives,* HMSO.

BRANNEN, PETER, ERIC BATSTONE, DEREK FATCHETT and PHILIP WHITE, (1975), *The Worker Directors,* Hutchinson.

BRANNEN, PETER and CHRIS CASWILL, (1978), 'Changes in Law and Value', in DENIS GREGORY, (ed.), *Work Organisation, Swedish Experience and British Context,* SSRC.

BRANNEN, PETER, (1983), 'Worker Directors — an Approach to Analysis: The Case of the British Steel Corporation', in COLIN CROUCH and FRANK A. HELLER (eds.), *International Yearbook of Organisational Democracy,* Wiley.

BRAVERMAN, HARRY, (1974), *Labor and Monopoly Capital,* New York, Monthly Review Press.

BRISTOW, EDWARD, (1974), 'Profit Sharing, Socialism and Labour Unrest' in KENNETH D. BROWN (ed.), *Essays in Anti-Labour History,* Macmillan.

BROOKES, CHRISTOPHER, (1979), *Boards of Directors in British Industry,* Research Paper No. 7, Department of Employment, London.

BROWN, R. K., (1978), 'From Donovan to where? Interpretations of Industrial Relations in Britain since 1968', *British Journal of Sociology,* Vol. XXIX, No. 4.

BROWN, R. K., (1981), 'Sociologists and Industry — in Search of a Distinctive Competence', *Sociological Review,* Vol. 29, No. 2.

BROWN, RICHARD and PETER BRANNEN, (1970), 'Social Relations and Social Perspectives amongst Shipbuilding Workers — Part Two', *Sociology,* Vol. 4, No. 2.

Workers' Self Management in Industry – the West ...York, Praeger.

...1), *Capitalism and Modern Social Theory,* ...ss.

...ological model of inflation', *Sociology,* Vol. 15,

..., 'Social Inequality and Social Integration in ...ODERBURN (ed.), *Poverty, Inequality and Class* ...versity Press.

...'Industrial Relations in Great Britain: a critique ...E and CLEMENTS (eds.), *Trade Unions under*

...'The Current Inflation: Towards a Sociological ...CH and JOHN H. GOLDTHORPE (eds.), *The* ...ion, Martin Robertson.

...CKWOOD, F. BECHHOFER and J. PLATT, (1969), ...*Class Structure,* Cambridge University Press.

...eories of Poverty and Unemployment: Orthodox, ...Market Perspectives,* Lexington, D.C. Heath.

...usiness Leadership in the Large Corporation,* Los ...alifornia Press.

...'Metaphysical Pathos and the Theory of ...*Political Science Review,* Vol. 49, pp. 496-507.

...Scanlon plan – a case study', *British Journal of* ...IX, No. 3.

...EK FATCHETT, (1974), *Worker Participation:* ...erformance,* Institute of Personnel Management.

...6), 'The board of directors, company policy and ...R. BEBIN (ed.), *Handbook of Work Organisation* ...nd McNally.

...GERRY HUNNIUS, (1981), *New Patterns of Work* ...ay,* Oslo, Universitetsforlaget.

...979), *Occupational Segregation,* Research Paper ...nployment, London.

...P. BROOKS, (1980), 'Change and Renewal: Joint ...y', *Employment Gazette,* April.

...D SMITH, (1981), 'Employee involvement outside ...ment Gazette,* June.

...), *Social Mobility,* Fontana.

..., (1977), *The Economics of Co-determination,*

...OLM WILDERS, PETER ABELL, and MALCOLM ...do the British want from Participation and Industrial ...rman Foundation.

...Work and the Nature of Man,* Cleveland, World

...NER and D. SYNDERMAN, (1959), *The Motivation* ...iley.

BROWN, R. K., M. M. CURRAN and J. M. COUSINS, (1983), *Changing Attitudes to Work,* Research Paper, Department of Employment, London.
BROWN, W. R. and N. A. HOWELL-EVERSON, (1950), *Industrial Democracy at Work: a Factual Survey,* Pitman.
BULLOCK, LORD, (1977), *Report of the Committee of Inquiry on Industrial Democracy,* Cmnd 6706, HMSO.
BULMER, ESMOND, (1982), 'Industrial Democracy', *Industrial Participation,* December.
BURNS, TOM, (1969), 'On the plurality of social systems' in BURNS T. (ed.), *Industrial Man,* Penguin.
BURNS, T. and G. M. STALKER, (1961), *The Management of Innovation,* Tavistock.
BURNS, TOM R., LARS ERIK KARLSSON and VELJKO RUS, (1979), *Work and Power – The Liberation of Work and the Control of Political Power,* Sage.

CAMPBELL, A. C., G. KEEN, NORMAN and R. OAKSHOTTE, (1977), *Worker Owners: the Mondragon Experiment,* Anglo-German Foundation.
CAREY, ALEX (1967), 'The Hawthorne Studies: A Radical Criticism', *American Sociological Review,* Vol. 32, No. 3.
CARTER, MICHAEL P., (1975), 'Teenage Workers, a Second Chance at 18', in PETER BRANNEN (ed.), *Entering the World of Work: Some Sociological Perspectives,* HMSO.
CAVES, RICHARD, E. and Associates, (1968), *Britain's Economic Prospects,* The Brookings Institution, Washington, D.C.
C.B.I., (1973), *The Responsibilities of British Companies,* Confederation of British Industry.
C.B.I., (1979), *Guidelines for Action on Employee Involvement,* Confederation of British Industry.
CHANDLER, A. D., (1962), *Strategy and Structure: Chapters in the History of the Industrial Enterprise,* Cambridge, Mass., MIT Press.
CHELL, ELIZABETH and DEREK COX, (1979), 'Worker Directors and Collective Bargaining', *Industrial Relations Journal,* Vol. 10, No. 3.
CHELL, ELIZABETH, (1980), 'Worker Directors on the Board – Four Case Studies', *Employee Relations,* Vol. 2, No. 6.
CHILD, J., (1969), *British Management Thought,* Allen and Unwin.
C.I.R., (1973), *Industrial Relations at Establishment Level: A Statistical Survey,* Commission on Industrial Relations, Study No. 2, HMSO.
CLARK, JON, HEINZ HARTMANN, CHRISTOPHER LAU, DAVID WINCHESTER, (1980), *Trade Unions, National Politics and Economic Management,* Anglo-German Foundation.
CLARKE, R. O., D. J. FATCHETT and B. C. ROBERTS, (1972), *Workers' Participation in Management in Britain,* Heinemann.
CLEGG, CHRIS W., NIGEL NICHOLSON, GILL URSELL, PAUL R. BLYTON and TOBY D. WALL, (1978), 'Managers' Attitudes towards Industrial Democracy', *Industrial Relations Journal,* Vol. 9, No. 3, pp. 4-17.
CLEGG, H. A., (1960), *A New Approach to Industrial Democracy,* Oxford, Blackwell.
CLEGG, H. A., (1980), *The Changing System of Industrial Relations in Great Britain,* Oxford, Blackwell.

CLEGG, H. A. and T. E. CHESTER, (1954), 'Joint Consultation', in A. FLANDERS and H. A. CLEGG (ed.), *The System of Industrial Relations in Great Britain*, Oxford, Blackwell.

CLIFTON, RICHARD, (1978), *The Economic Implications of Industrial Democracy*, Government Economic Service Working Paper No. 7.

COATES, KEN, (1976), *The New Worker Cooperatives*, Nottingham, Spokesman Books.

COATES, KEN and ANTHONY TOPHAM, (1968), *Industrial Democracy in Great Britain*, MacGibbon and Kee; republished under the title, *Workers' Control*, Panther, 1970.

COATES, KEN and TONY TOPHAM, (1974), *The New Unionism*, Penguin.

COCH, L. and J. R. P. FRENCH, (1948), 'Overcoming resistance to change', *Human Relations*, 1, pp 512–32.

COLE, G. D. H., (1972), *Self Government in Industry*, Hutchinson.

COMMISO, ELEN TURKISH, (1979) *Workers' Control under Plan and Market: Implications for Yugoslav Self Management*, Yale University Press.

CONTE, M. and T. TANNENBAUM, (1978), 'Employee owned companies: is the difference measurable?', *Monthly Labour Review*, July, Washington.

COTGROVE, S. F., JACK DUNHAM, CLIVE VAMPLEW, (1971), *The Nylon Spinners*, Allen and Unwin.

CREIGH, STEPHEN, NIGEL DONALDSON and ERIC HAWTHORN, (1981), 'A stake in the firm — employee financial involvement in Britain', *Employment Gazette*, May.

CRESSEY, PETER, JOHN ELDRIDGE, JOHN MacINNES, and GEOFFREY NORRIS, (1981), *Industrial Democracy and Participation: a Scottish survey*, Research Paper No. 28, Department of Employment.

CRONIN, JAMES, E. (1979), *Industrial Conflict in Modern Britain*, Croom Helm.

CRONIN, JAMES, (1980), 'Stages, cycles and insurgencies; the economics of unrest', in T. K. HOPKINS and I. WALLERSTEIN (eds.), *The Processes of the World System*, Sage.

CROUCH, COLIN, (1978), 'Inflation and political organisation of economic interests', in FRED HIRSCH and JOHN H. GOLDTHORPE (eds.), *The Political Economy of Inflation*, Martin Robertson.

CROUCH, COLIN and FRANK A. HELLER, (1983), *International Yearbook of Organisational Democracy*, New York, Wiley.

DANIEL, W. W., (1979), 'Understanding employee behaviour in its context,' in J. CHILD (ed.), *Man and Organisation*, Allen and Unwin.

DANIEL, W. W. and NEIL MILLWARD, (1983), *Workplace Industrial Relations in Britain*, Heinemann.

DERBER, M., (1970), *The American Idea of Industrial Democracy, 1865–1965*, University of Illinois Press.

DERRICK, P. and J. F. PHIPPS, (1960), *Co-ownership, Co-operation and Control*, Longman.

DE VYLDER, STEFAN, (1981), review of ESPINOSA and ZIMBALIST, (1978), in *Economic and Industrial Democracy*, Vol. 2, No. 1.

DONOVAN, LORD, (1968), *Report of the Royal Commission on Trades Unions and Employers' Associations, 1965–1968*, HMSO.

DOWLING, M. J., J. F. B. GOODMAN, D. A. GOTTING, and J. D. HYMAN,

(1981),
manufa
Employ

DUBEY, V
Johns H

EATON,
Relation

EDELSTE
Cooper

EDWARDS
Segment

ELDRIDGE
ELDRIDGE
Discussi
and Part

ELLIOT, J
Cooper

ELLIS, T. a
perspect

ELVANDER
Democra

EMERY, FR
Martinu

ESPINOSA,
Democra
Academi

FLANDERS,
FLANDERS,
FLANDERS,
FORD, G. V
Industria
Research

FOX, A., (19
in JOHN C

FOX, A., (19
FOX, ALAN,
FOX, A. and
from Dor
Vol. 7, No

FRENCH, J. I
in a Norw

FRIEDMAN,

GALLIE, DU
University

GAMBLE, A.
State, Mac

GARSON, DA
managemen

GARSON, DAVID G. (19
European experience,

GIDDENS, ANTHONY
Cambridge Universi

GILBERT, M., (1981), '
No. 2.

GOLDTHORPE, J. H., (
Modern Britain' in
Structure, Cambridge

GOLDTHORPE, J. H., (1
of reformism' in Cl
Capitalism, Fontana.

GOLDTHORPE, J. H., (
Account' in FRED
Political Economy of

GOLDTHORPE, J. H., D
The Affluent Worker

GORDON, D. M., (1972
Radical and Dual La

GORDON, R. A., (1966
Angeles, University

GOULDNER, A., (195
Bureaucracy', Ameri

GRAY, R. B., (1971), 'I
Industrial Relations,

GUEST, DAVID and
Individual Control an

GUSTAVSEN, BJORN, (
industrial democracy
and Society, Chicago

GUSTAVSEN, BJORN a
Reform: the case of N

HAKIM, CATHERINE,
no. 9, Department of

HAWES, W. R. and C.
Consultation in Indu

HAWES, W. R. and DA
manufacturing', Emp

HEATH, ANTHONY, (1

HEATHFIELD, DAVID
Macmillan.

HELLER, FRANK, MA
WARNER, (1979), Wl
Democracy?, Anglo-C

HERZBERG, F., (1966)
Publishing Company

HERZBERG, F., B. MO
to Work, New York,

HESPE, GEORGE and TOBY WALL, (1976), 'The Demand for Participation among Employees', *Human Relations,* Vol. 29, No. 5.

HILL, STEVEN, (1980), 'Economic and Industrial Transformation: the waves of social consequences from technological change' in P. BOREDAM and G. DOW (eds.), *Work and Inequality,* Vol. 1., Macmillan.

HILL, STEVEN, (1981), *Competition and Control at Work,* Heinemann.

HMSO, (1950), *Industrial Relations Handbook Supplement No. 3,* HMSO.

HUNTER, LAWRENCE, (1980), 'Some Economic Aspects of Industrial Democracy', *Industrial Relations Journal,* Vol. 11, No. 3.

I.D.E., (1981), *Industrial Democracy in Europe,* Oxford, Clarendon Press.

I.E.A., (1977), *'Can Workers Manage?',* Institute of Economic Affairs, Hobart Paper 77.

I.L.O., (1981), *Workers' participation in decisions within undertakings,* Geneva, International Labour Organisation.

I.P.A., (1982), 'Industrial Participation – A national framework', *Industrial Participation,* Autumn.

I.R.R.R., (1978), 'Industrial Relations in Worker Cooperatives', *Industrial Relations Review and Report,* March.

JACKSON, MICHAEL, P., (1982), *Trade Unions,* Longman.

JAY, PETER (1977a), *The Workers' Co-operative Economy,* Manchester Statistical Society.

JAY, PETER (1977b), 'The 'orse 'e knows about a bit', *The Times,* Jan. 27.

JOHNSON, ANA GUTIERREZ and WILLIAM FOOTE WHYTE, (1977), 'The Mondragon System of Worker Production Cooperatives', *Industrial and Labour Relations Review,* Vol. 31, No. 1.

JONES, DEREK, C., (1976), 'British Producer Cooperatives' in KEN COATES (ed.), *The New Worker Cooperatives,* Nottingham, Spokesman Books.

JONES, DEREK, (1979), 'U.S. Producer Cooperatives: the record to date', *Industrial Relations,* Vol. 18, No. 3.

KELLY, JOHN, (1980), 'The Costs of Job Redesign: a preliminary analysis', *Industrial Relations Journal,* Vol. 11, No. 3.

KELLY, JOHN E. and CHRIS W. CLEGG, (1981), *Autonomy and Control at the Workplace: contexts for job redesign,* Croom Helm.

KNIGHT, I. B., (1979), *Company Organisation and Worker Participation,* HMSO.

KOLAGA, J., (1965), *Workers' Councils: The Yugoslav Experience,* Tavistock.

KRECKEL, R., (1980), 'Unequal Opportunity Structure and Labour Market Segmentation, *Sociology,* Vol. 14, No. 4.

KUHNE, ROBERT J., (1980), *Co-determination in Business: worker representatives in the boardroom,* New York, Praeger.

LATTA, G. W., (1979), *Profit Sharing, Employee Stock Ownership, Savings, and Asset Formation Plans in the Western World,* Pennsylvania University Press.

LEVINSON, H., (1974), *Industry's Democratic Revolution,* Allen and Unwin.

LINDHOLME, ROLF, (1977), 'On Success and Failure' in DENIS GREGORY (ed.), *Work Organisation – Swedish Experience and British Context,* Social Science Research Council.

LIPSET, S., M. A. TROW and S. J. COLEMAN, (1956), *Union Democracy,* New York, Free Press.

LISCHERON, JOE and TOBY D. WALL, (1975), 'Attitudes Towards Participation among Local Authority Employees', *Human Relations,* Vol. 28, No. 6.

LLOYD, P. A., (1976), *Incentive Payment Schemes,* British Institute of Management.

LONG, RICHARD, (1978), 'The Relative Effects of Share Ownership vs. Control on Job Attitudes in an Employee-owned Company', *Human Relations,* Vol. 31, No. 9.

LOVERIDGE, RAY, (1980), 'What is participation? A review of the literature and some methodological problems', *British Journal of Industrial Relations,* Vol. XVIII. No. 3.

LOVERIDGE, RAY, PAUL LLOYD, and GEOFF BROAD, *Workplace Control and Codetermination,* Research Paper, Department of Employment, London (forthcoming).

LOVERIDGE, R. and A. L. MOK, (1979), *Theories of Labour Market Segmentation: A critique,* The Hague, Nijhoff.

LUKES, STEPHEN, (1974), *Power – a radical view,* Macmillan.

McCARTHY, W. E. J., (1966), *The Role of Shop Stewards in British Industrial Relations,* Royal Commission on Trades Unions and Employers' Associations, Research Paper No. 1, HMSO.

McCARTHY, W. E. J. and N. D. ELLIS, (1973), *Management by Agreement,* Hutchinson.

McGREGOR, D., (1960), *The Human Side of Enterprise,* New York, McGraw-Hill

MALLET, S., (1969), *La Nouvelle Class Ouvrière,* Paris, Seuil; translated as *The New Working Class,* Nottingham, Spokesman Books (1975).

MALLET, S., (1975), *Essays on the New Working Class,* St Louis, Telos Press.

MANLEY P. and R. SAWBRIDGE, (1980), 'Women at Work', Lloyds Bank Review, No. 135, pp. 29-40.

MARCHINGTON, MICK, (1980), *Responses to Participation at Work,* Farnborough, Gower.

MARSDEN, DAVID, (1978), *Industrial Democracy and Industrial Control in West Germany, France and Great Britain,* Research Paper No. 4, Department of Employment, London.

MARSH, A. K., and E. E. COKER, (1963), 'Shop Steward Organisation in the Engineering Industry', *British Journal of Industrial Relations,*Vol. 52, No. 1.

MARSHALL, T. H., (1963), 'Citizenship and Social Class' in MARSHALL (ed.) *Sociology at the Crossroads,* Heinemann.

MARTIN, JEAN and CERIDWEN ROBERTS, (1983), *Women and Employment,* HMSO.

MARTIN, RODERICK, (1977), *The Sociology of Power,* Routledge and Kegan Paul.

MASLOW, A. H., (1943), 'A theory of human motivation', *Psychological Review,* no. 50, pp. 320-96.

McKERSIE, R. B. and L. C. HUNTER, (1973), *Pay, Productivity and Collective Bargaining*, Macmillan.

MERTON, R. K., (1957), 'Bureaucratic Structure and Personality' in MERTON (ed.), *Reader in Bureaucracy*, Glencoe, Free Press.

METCALF, D., (1977), 'Unions policy and relative wages in Britain', *British Journal of Industrial Relations*, Vol. XV, No. 2.

METZGER, B. L., (1975), *Profit Sharing in 38 Large Companies*, Vol. 1, Profit Sharing Research Foundation, Evanston, Illinois.

METZGER, B. L., (1981), 'On Profit Sharing in the U.S. and the philosophy of profit sharing', *Economic and Industrial Democracy*, Vol. 2, No. 1, pp. 97-102.

MICHELS, R., (1962), *Political Parties*, New York, Free Press.

MILLIBAND, RALPH, (1978), 'A State of De-subordination', *British Journal of Industrial Sociology*, Vol. XXIX, No. 4.

MILLWARD, NEIL and JOHN McQUEENEY, (1981), *Company Take Overs, Management Organisation and Industrial Relations*, Manpower Paper No. 16, HMSO.

MONTGOMERY, DAVID, (1980), *Workers' Control in America*, Cambridge University Press.

MULVEY, CHARLES, (1978), *The Economic Analysis of Trade Unions*, Martin Robertson.

NATIONAL INSTITUTE FOR INDUSTRIAL PSYCHOLOGY, (1952), *Joint Consultation in British Industry*, Staples Press.

NEWMAN, OTTO, (1981), *The Challenge to Corporatism*, Macmillan.

NICHOLS, THEO, (1969), *Ownership, Control and Ideology*, Allen and Unwin.

NICHOLS, THEO, (1980), *Capital and Labour*, Fontana.

NICHOLS, THEO and HUW BEYNON, (1977), *Living with Capitalism*, Routledge and Kegan Paul.

NORTHCOTT, JIM, (1980), *Microprocessors in Manufactured Products*, Policy Studies Institute.

OAKESHOTT, ROBERT, (1978a), *The Case for Workers Co-ops*, Routledge and Kegan Paul.

OAKESHOTT, ROBERT, (1978b), 'Industrial Cooperatives; the middle way', *Lloyds Bank Review* 127.

OBRADOVIC, JOSIP, (1975), 'Workers' participation: who participates?' *Industrial Relations*, Vol. 14, No. 1.

OBRADOVIC, JOSIP, (1978), 'Sources of Management Power in Self-Managing Organisations', *Industrial Democracy: International Views*, S.S.R.C. Industrial Relations Research Unit.

PAHL, R. E. and J. T. WINKLER, (1974), 'The Economic Elite' in P. STANWORTH and A. GIDDENS (eds.), *Elites and Power in British Society*, Cambridge University Press.

PANITCH, L., (1980), 'Recent theorisations of corporatism: reflections on a growth industry', *British Journal of Sociology*, Vol. XXXI, No. 2.

PARKER, S. R., R. K. BROWN, J. CHILD and M. A. SMITH, (1980), *The Sociology of Industry*, Allen and Unwin.

PARRIS, HENRY, (1973), *Staff Relations in the Civil Service – Fifty Years of Whitleyism*, Allen and Unwin.

PARSONS, TALCOTT, (1964), Introduction to *Max Weber: The Theory of Social and Economic Organisations,* New York, Free Press.

PATEMAN, C., (1970), *Participation and Democratic Theory,* Cambridge University Press.

PATEMAN, CAROLE, (1975), 'A Contribution to the Political Theory of Organisational Democracy', *Administration and Society,* Vol. 7, No. 1.

PATEMAN, CAROLE, (1983), 'Some Reflections on Participation and Democratic Theory' in COLIN CROUCH and FRANK A HELLER (eds.), *International Yearbook of Organisational Democracy,* Wiley.

PELLING, HENRY, (1971), *A History of British Trade Unionism,* Pelican.

PERROW, C., (1970), *Organisational Analysis,* Tavistock.

PIORE, MICHAEL J. (1980), 'Economic Fluctuation, Job Security, and Labour Market Duality in Italy, France and the United States', *Politics and Society,* Vol. 9, No. 4.

POOLE, MICHAEL, (1978), *Workers' Participation in Industry,* Routledge and Kegan Paul.

POOLE, MICHAEL and ROGER MANSFIELD (eds.), (1980), *Managerial Roles in Industrial Relations,* Farnborough, Gower.

POOLE, MICHAEL, (1980), 'Managers, Industrial Democracy and Control' in MICHAEL POOLE and ROGER MANSFIELD (eds.), *Managerial Roles in Industrial Relations,* Farnborough, Gower.

POOLE, MICHAEL, (1981), 'Industrial Democracy in Comparative Perspective' in ROGER MANSFIELD and MICHAEL POOLE (eds.), *International Perspectives on Management Organisation,* Farnborough, Gower.

POOLE, MICHAEL, (1982), 'Theories of Industrial Democracy', *Sociological Review,* Vol. 30, No. 2.

PRAIS, Z., (1976), *The Evolution of Giant Firms in Britain,* Cambridge University Press.

PRIBICEVIC, B, (1959), *The Shop Stewards' Movement and Workers' Control,* Oxford, Blackwell.

RADICE, GILES, (1982), 'Industrial Democracy', *Industrial Society,* Dec.

RAMSEY, HARVIE, (1976), 'Participation: The Shop Floor View', *British Journal of Industrial Relations,* Vol. XIV, No. 2.

RAMSAY, H., (1977), 'Cycles of Control', *Sociology,* Vol. 11, No.3.

RAMSAY, HARVIE, (1980), 'Phantom Participation: patterns of power and conflict', *Industrial Relations Journal,* Vol. 11, No. 3.

RAMSAY, H., (1983), 'Evolution or Cycle? Workers' participation in the 1970s and 1980s', in COLIN CROUCH and FRANK A. HELLER (eds.), *International Yearbook of Organisational Democracy,* Wiley, 1983.

REDFORD, ARTHUR, (1960), *The Economic History of England 1760-1860,* Longman.

REICH, M., D. M. GORDON and R. C. EDWARDS, (1973), 'A Theory of Labour Market Segmentation', *A.E.R. (Papers and Proceedings)* 63.

ROBERTS, BENJAMIN, C., (1979), *Towards Industrial Democracy,* Croom Helm.

ROCA, SANTIAGO and DIDIER RETOUR, (1981), 'Participation in Enterprise Management: Bogged Down Concepts', *Economic and Industrial Democracy,* Vol. 2, No. 1.

ROSE, M., (1975), *Industrial Behaviour,* Allen Lane.

RUS, VELJKO, (1970), 'Influence Structure and Yugoslav Enterprise', *Industrial Relations,* Vol. 9, No. 2.

RUSSEL, RAYMOND, ARTHUR HOCHNER, and STEWART E. PERRY, (1979), 'Participation, Influence and Worker Ownership', *Industrial Relations,* Vol. 18, No. 3.

RYAN, PAUL, (1981), 'Segmentation, Duality and Internal Labour Market' in F. WILKINSON (ed.), *The Dynamics of Labour Market Segmentation,* Academic Press.

SANDERSON, GEORGE and FREDERICK STAPENHURST, (1979), *Industrial Democracy Today – A new role for labour,* Toronto, McGraw-Hill Ryerson.

S.D.P., (1982), *Democracy at Work: a policy for partnership in industry,* Green Paper No. 6., Social Democratic Party.

SMITH, C. T. B., RICHARD CLIFTON, PETER MAKEHAM, STEVEN CREIGH, R. V. BURN, (1978), *Strikes in Britain,* Manpower Paper No. 15, HMSO.

SMITH, DAVID J. (1981), *Unemployment and Racial Minorities,* Policy Studies Institute.

SMITH, MICHAEL R., (1982), 'Accounting for Inflation in Britain', *British Journal of Sociology,* Vol. XXXIII, No. 3.

SORGE, ARNT, (1976), 'The Evolution of Industrial Democracy in the Countries of The European Community', *British Journal of Industrial Relations,* Vol. XIV, No. 3.

STANWORTH, P. and A. GIDDENS, (1974), 'An economic elite: a demographic profile of company chairmen', in STANWORTH and GIDDENS (eds.), *Elites and Power in British Society,* Cambridge University Press.

STINCHCOMBE, ARTHUR L., (1959), 'Bureaucratic and craft administration of production', *Administrative Science Quarterly,* No. 4.

TANNENBAUM, R., I. R. WESCHIER and F. MASSARIK, (1961), *Leadership and Organisation: a behavioural science approach,* New York, McGraw-Hill.

TAYLOR, F. W., (1947), *Scientific Management,* New York, Harper.

THOMPSON, E. P., (1980), *The Making of the English Working Class,* Penguin.

THORNLEY, JENNY, (1981), *Workers' Cooperatives,* Heinemann.

TOURAINE, A., (1962), 'An Historical Theory in the Evolution of Industrial Skills', in C. R. WALKER (ed.), *Modern Technology and Civilisation,* New York, McGraw-Hill.

TOURAINE, ALAIN, (1971), *The Post-Industrial Society,* New York, Random House.

TOWERS, BRIAN, DEREK COX and ELIZABETH CHELL, (1981), 'Do Worker Directors Work?'. *Employment Gazette,* Sept. 1981.

TOWERS, BRIAN, ELIZABETH CHELL and DEREK COX, *Worker Directors in Private Industry in Britain,* Research Paper, Department of Employment, London (forthcoming).

T.U.C., (1944), *Interim Report on Post-War Reconstruction,* Trades Union Congress.

T.U.C., (1966), *Trade Unionism* (evidence to the Donovan Commission), Trades Union Congress.

T.U.C., (1974), *Industrial Democracy* (report to the TUC General Council), Trades Union Congress.

TRIST, E. L., G. W. HIGGIN, H. MURRAY, and A. B. POLLOCK, (1963), *Organisational Choice,* Tavistock.

URSELL, GILL, TOBY WALL, NIGEL NICHOLSON and CHRIS CLEGG, (1976), 'Shop Stewards' Attitudes towards Industrial Democracy', *Industrial Relations Journal,* Vol. 10, No. 4.

VANEK, JAROSLAV, (1975), *Self Management — economic liberation of man,* Penguin.

WACHTEL, HOWARD M., (1973), *Workers' Management and Workers' Wages in Yugoslavia — The Theory and Practice of Participatory Socialism,* Cornell University Press.

WALKER, K. F., (1974). 'Workers' participation in management — problems, practice and prospects', *International Institute for Labour Studies Bulletin,* No. 12.

WALL, TOBY D. and JOSEPH A. LISCHERON, (1977), *Worker Participation — a critique of the literature and some fresh evidence,* McGraw-Hill.

WATSON, TONY J., (1980), *Sociology, Work and Industry,* Routledge and Kegan Paul.

WEBB, SIDNEY and BEATRICE, (1920), *A Constitution for the Socialist Commonwealth of Great Britain,* Longman; reprinted in COATES and TOPHAM, (1968), pp. 66-72.

WEBER, MAX, (1978), *Economy and Society,* University of California Press.

WEDDERBURN, D., (1965), 'Facts and Theories of the Welfare State' in R. MILLIBAND and J. SAVILLE (eds.), *The Socialist Register,* Merlin Press.

WHITE, P. J., (1980), 'Share-ownership Schemes for Employees — Proposals and Projects', *Managerial and Decision Economics,* No. 3.

WINKLER, J. T., (1977), 'The corporatist economy: theory and administration' in R. SCASE (ed.), *Industrial Society: Class, Cleavage and Control,* Allen and Unwin.

WOOD, STEPHEN, (1981), *The Degradation of Work: skill, deskilling and the labour process,* Hutchinson.

WOOD, STEVEN and JOHN KELLY, (1978), 'Towards a critical management science', *Journal of Management Studies,* Vol. 15, No. 1.

WOODWARD, J., (1965), *Industrial Organisation,* Oxford University Press.

WRAGG, RICHARD and JAMES ROBERTSON, (1978), *Post-War Trends in Employment, Productivity, Output, Labour Costs and Prices by Industry in the United Kingdom,* Research Paper no. 3, Department of Employment, London.

Index